The Canadian's Guide to Personal Finance for Singles

by Julie Shipley-Strickland
and Bryan Borzykowski

WILEY

Publisher's Acknowledgments

Authors: Julie Shipley-Strickland and Bryan Borzykowski

Senior Acquisitions Editor: Tracy Boggier

Project Manager: Susan Pink

Production Editor: Tamilmani Varadharaj

Cover Photo: © ~Userba9fe9ab_931/ Getty Images; © whatstock/ Shutterstock

The Canadian's Guide to Personal Finance for Singles

Published by John Wiley & Sons, Inc.
111 River St.
Hoboken, NJ 07030-5774
www.wiley.com

For general information on our other products and services, please contact our Business Development Department in the U.S. at 317-572-3205.

Library of Congress Control Number: 2022938484

ISBN 978-1-119-89320-2

SKY10033814_061322

Table of Contents

1

Embracing Your Single Status

Whether you've been single for years or are just embarking on your one-person journey, know that you're not alone. As this chapter lays out, singlehood in Canada is the fastest growing relationship status in the country. Sure, being single isn't always easy in a world that's mostly designed for families of two (or more), but have no fear, we can help you become a lot more confident with your money.

This book is not meant to reinvent the personal finance wheel, and you don't need to be a Rotman School of Management grad to understand it. If you know anything about money, you'll recognize a lot of what we talk about here. If you know nothing about dollars and cents, this book will be a good primer, though consider picking up *Personal Finance For Canadians*, another Wiley book, to supplement your reading.

The difference between this book and other more general personal finance tomes is that a lot of financial concepts, such as saving in a registered retirement savings plan or buying life insurance, are written for couples and families. As a single person, your needs may be different. You might have different life and retirement goals and should have different tax and savings strategies than those of a couple.

The single life is also different depending on how you came to live alone. Have you been single your entire life? Did you recently get divorced? Did your spouse pass away? While all these paths lead to the same relationship status, each has its own financial challenges.

Whether you've been single for years are just embarking on your one-person journey, know that you're not alone. As this chapter lays out, singlehood in Canada is the fastest growing relationship status in the country.

The Single Household Takeover

According to the 2016 census (the last time these numbers were calculated) 28.2 percent of Canadian households were considered one-person households. That's more than any other type of arrangement, including couples with children, which accounted for 26.5 percent of households.

Another interesting, though not entirely surprising, finding: More women than men live alone, with the former accounting for 53.7 percent of one-person households in 2016. Senior women are also more likely to live alone than older men.

People are single for plenty of reasons, but here are a few:

- Society has become much more accepting of different kinds of relationships and household arrangements.
- More women are working and therefore more financially self-sufficient than they were decades ago.
- With no-fault divorce, introduced in Canada in 1986, you don't need a reason to break up. That's made it easier for couples to separate.
- Women still live longer than men — 83.9 years versus 79.8 years.

If you still need some convincing that single status is all the rage, take a look at these 2021 figures from Statistics Canada:

- 38,246,108 people are living in Canada, including 6,018,084 children.
- 39 percent of the population identify as single.
- 5.24 percent of the population are classified as widowed.
- 7.16 percent say they are divorced.

Living Life on Your Own Terms

For many people, being single means starting over. They have to come up with new dreams and rethink the way they live, where they live, and who they want to spend the rest of their life with. Many people will be thrilled to be alone — they could be getting a new lease on life, especially if they've been in a difficult relationship. Others will be devastated, particularly after a loved one passes away or a sudden separation.

Newfound singledom tends to come with all kinds of emotions — pain, confusion, sadness, joy, and other more nuanced feelings. It's important to understand and work through these emotions because they can make it difficult to move forward financially and can negatively affect your decision making. Dealing with what's on your mind is a key part of handling what's in your wallet.

Facing Financial Realities

Generally, two incomes are better than one. If you're making \$150,000 and your spouse is making \$100,000, you have \$250,000 to spend between the two of you. That can get you a bigger house, a more luxurious vacation, and a larger collective nest egg. And living with a partner has tax and investment benefits too.

Single people often end up paying more for things, such as gym memberships, which offer discounts for spouses, and cell phone plans, which usually come with a family plan. One U.K. study found that all these extra expenses total £2,000, which is about $3,300 Canadian.

But while some things are pricier, you can still become more financial independent when you're on your own. How, you ask? In many cases, one spouse spends more than the other — if you're the frugal partner in a divorce, you may now find it easier to save. If you've always been single? Well, you're already used to doing whatever you want with your money.

Staying with the single life

In some ways, it's easier financially if you've always been single. You will have had to manage your money from the start, figure out how to budget for one, and navigate everything from taxes, insurance, and investing by yourself.

However, this doesn't mean you can't do a better job with your finances. In fact, many single people continue to save and spend in their 40s the same way they did in their 20s. If you don't have children putting pressure on your wallet or a spouse or partner to consider in your money plans, it's easy to continue doing the same thing year after year.

But as you get older, your life will likely be more complicated financially. You should start thinking about ways to save for retirement. If you're a homeowner, you need to put aside enough for inevitable house repairs and property taxes. Maybe you want to start your own business. Also consider who you might want to spend your golden years with, whether those people are close friends or other family members. None of this is difficult to figure out, especially if you're accustomed to being on your own; it can even be fun to think about how you want to spend your money in the future.

Starting again after a separation

Divorce can be extremely difficult but also freeing, depending on what kind of relationship you're leaving. Still, no matter how you feel about your partner, separating from a spouse is a major life event that will likely affect your finances.

The biggest financial change with divorce is that you're now going from two incomes to one — or one income to none. You might have to find paid work after years of not being in the workforce. Or if you earn less than your ex-spouse, you might need to find other sources of income to maintain a certain lifestyle, especially if you aren't getting spousal or child support.

Divorce can be messy and complicated, and it can make your money messy and complicated, too. There may be lawyers to pay, joint accounts to close, new solo accounts to open, wills to update, insurance beneficiaries to change, and so on.

But divorce is also a time for renewal —you're starting your life over again but this time on your own terms. You, and only you, can decide where to spend your money, what investments to purchase, who to spend time with, and where to travel. As we explain in more detail in Chapter 6, you'll have a lot of work to do to set up your new financial life, including dividing assets and figuring out how to potentially live on less. But with some budgeting and financial planning, you can not only sort out these money issues but also end up in a better financial place.

Building back when bereaved

Out of all the ways to find yourself single, death is probably the toughest to deal with emotionally but could be the easiest to handle financially. If your spouse took out a life insurance policy, that payment could give you some time to get back on your feet.

You would also be entitled to their investments, such as their RRSP or TFSA, potentially part of their pension, and even some of their Canada Pension Plan (CPP) payments. Depending on those amounts and your age, you could be well taken care of for a long time to come.

However, you still have plenty of financial issues to think about. For instance, there could be taxes to pay on your partner's income if they were still working at the time of their death or on investments that don't roll over to a spouse tax-free, such as stocks held in a non-registered account. Maybe you decide you don't need as much room and choose to sell your home. You might need to close accounts and open other ones, figure out how to pay the bills on your own, and start thinking about how best to save for retirement.

As mentioned, the emotions that come with a loss are the hardest part about bereavement. The last thing most people want to do is sort out life insurance policies, open bank accounts, or figure out how to budget— it's hard enough to get up every day. While you should take the time you need to grieve, wait too long and you could find yourself veering far off your financial path. You may have to find a way to deal with your money and your mind in tandem, which is where financial professionals can help. Spend time sorting out your finances and you'll have one less thing to worry about.

Gaining Confidence in Managing Your Money

Financial success comes down to confidence. If you know what you're doing, you'll feel better about the moves you'll need to make, whether it's splurging on a big-ticket item, deciding what investment accounts to use first, or figuring out how much to earn to make a one-income household work.

The only way to get that confidence is through education. Reading this book will certainty help — we cover a lot of core personal finance topics and also dig deeper into everything from investing to real estate to debt. In addition, we suggest the following for future reading:

- **MoneySense (**`www.moneysense.ca`**):** This site has long been the go-to source for Canadian personal finance. (Bryan got his start here, so it must be good.) MoneySense covers everything, including investing, insurance, home ownership, smart spending, and retirement. It should have answers to most of your burning money questions.
- **Globe and Mail, "Personal Finance" section (**`www.theglobeandmail.com/investing/personal-finance/`**):** The Globe and Mail's "Personal Finance" section is not only full of useful financial information but also has a lot of great columnists opining on everything from housing to financial advice. At the time of this writing, Canada's newspaper of record was beefing up its personal finance content.
- **Squakfox (**`www.squakfox.com/blog`**):** Kerry K. Taylor creates easy-to-consume personal finance content on this site. The journalist (and lovely human being if we do say so ourselves) offers a ton of practical advice on all kinds of topics, such as food waste, getting paid what you're worth, and reining in spending.
- **The Budgette (**`https://budgette.substack.com`**):** This blog, created by Canadian journalist Renee Sylvestre-Williams, is focused on personal finance for

single people. Renee, who posts about twice a month, covers all sorts of issues, such as taxes, investing, and why it feels so good to spend.

- **Investopedia (`www.investopedia.com`):** If there were such a thing as a personal finance bible, it would be Investopedia. This company, which got its start in Edmonton but is now based in New York, has articles on everything you could ever want to know about personal finance. See a finance term that you don't understand? Search for it on Investopedia, where you'll get an easy-to-understand definition. Keep this site handy as you get further along on your financial journey.
- **Young & Thrifty (`www.youngandthrifty.ca`):** This site has a lot of great personal finance information as well as articles on the topics younger Canadians care about. Read reviews on robo-adviosrs, get ideas on which credit cards are best, learn about tax return software, and more.

TIP

Financial education is the best path to financial freedom. The more confident you are, the easier it will be to navigate the single life.

No matter what you're doing with your life, you need money — and probably more and more of it — to do whatever it is you want to do. That's why it's important to develop a deeper understanding of financial issues. To that end, we show you how to determine your net worth (Chapter 2), find an advisor (Chapter 3), and create a budget (Chapter 4). Then we get into some of the more nitty-gritty areas of finance in later chapters.

2

Evaluating Your Financial Health

So, you're single and ready to mingle. Before you let loose, though, you need figure out where you stand financially. Only after you determine how much you're spending, how much you're saving, where your sources of income are coming from, and how much you're worth can you establish your life's goals, both financial and personal.

This chapter isn't about budgeting — that's the topic of Chapter 4. Instead, it's about determining your net worth and understanding cash flow. Why are these things important? Because it's helpful to have an idea of where you stand — with your cash, your assets, and your debts. Once you do that, you can more easily plan your life's next move.

You're More than Your Net Worth, but Calculate the Number Anyway

Ready to go on a fact-finding mission? It's not a Sherlock Holmes kind of adventure, but figuring out your net worth does take some sleuthing.

The first step is to gather as much information about your finances as you can. The process doesn't involve going through your spending habits with a fine-tooth comb — that task comes later, when you create a budget. (There are ways to get around some of the tedious work, as we describe in Chapter 4.)

You can create a basic *net worth statement* by adding all your assets and subtracting all your liabilities. The number left over is your net worth. Before you start digging into your dollars, though, you need to understand some basic financial terms.

Calculating your cash

Everyone understands cash, whether you have loonies and toonies or dollars and cents — anything you can pull out of your pocket and use to buy an ice cream. (Maybe use some of that cash to buy us Oreo Blizzards the next time you run into us?) However, when we talk about *cash,* we're not referring to the spare change tucked away between your couch cushions.

We're talking about money sitting in a chequing or savings account that's easy to access and free to use with a bank or debit card.

If you have a wad of cash under you mattrass, which, believe it or not, some people do, or $50,000 stashed away in a safety deposit box to remove at the apocalypse, include it in your total cash, too.

Assessing your assets

Over the course of your life, you've no doubt accumulated a lot of stuff. Some of that stuff is considered an *asset,* which is something you can resell for a profit or at least a good chunk of change.

Typically, when people talk about assets, they mean real estate and investments. Real estate assets include your house, your cottage, your condo in Florida, or the cute one-bedroom abode you rent out on Airbnb. Investment assets include money in your retirement accounts and pension, and shares in any private businesses, like a friend's restaurant. Other assets might include your car (we get into why and why not soon), jewellery, and collectibles.

Here's another way to think of assets: Do these items grow in value over time? Could you turn them into cash if you needed the money? If the answer to either question is yes, consider them assets.

Investigating your investments

Many different kinds of investments exist, but for most people, their investments consist of stocks, bonds, mutual funds, exchange-traded funds, or other securities in an investment account.

It's likely that you have one or more of the following, the value of which should get entered into your net worth statement:

- **Registered retirement savings plan (RRSP):** A registered retirement savings plan is the most popular retirement investment account, which means you probably have money in one. (We dive more into the different kinds of investments accounts in Chapter 3.)
- **Tax-free savings account (TFSA):** A tax-free savings account is the newest type of investment account, introduced in 2009. You may or may not have one of these, though more people are opening them up.
- **Registered retirement income fund (RRIF):** At some point between the ages of 55 and 72, you'll convert your registered retirement savings plan (RRSP) into a registered retirement income fund (RRIF). (You'll be forced to turn the RRSP into a RRIF the year you turn 72.) This account is for withdrawals only; you can't add more funds to it.

- **Registered education savings plan (RESP):** A registered education savings plan is an education savings account for children. If you're a younger single with kids, you might have one.
- **Locked-in retirement account (LIRA):** You might open a locked-in retirement account if you have a workplace pension and change jobs but need a place to keep your money. In most cases, you can't access these funds until retirement. LIRAs are also used by one spouse to keep pension assets received from the other spouse in the division of assets after a divorce.
- **Pension plan:** This plan is a workplace pension plan that grows over time but pays out only in retirement.
- **Non-registered account:** This type of investment account, unlike all the others in this list, doesn't shelter or defer tax.

Inspecting your income

When you think of *income,* what's the first thing that comes to mind? Your hefty salary, right? Well, it's more than that. Any dollars you earn is considered income. That includes the money you make from investments — whether it's from dividends, capital gains (the increase in the value of your investment), or bond distributions — rental income, and cash from government payments. However, when it comes to net worth statements, the bacon you're bringing home has no bearing on the final numbers. You need tally all your income sources when you create a cash flow statement (later in this chapter) and a budget (Chapter 4), but it's not part of your net worth statement.

Looking at your liabilities

A liability is just a fancy word for debt. *Liabilities* are any financial obligations that need to be repaid and would negatively affect you net worth. Following are some examples of liabilities:

- Credit card debt
- Line-of-credit debt
- Mortgage debt
- Car loan
- Student loan
- Loan from a family member that you must pay back
- The tab at your favourite deli (No? Just Bryan?)

These are all liabilities, in that you're liable to pay these things back. Most debt is included in a net worth statement. Ongoing expenses, such as your cable bill, are not considered liabilities and are not included in your calculations.

Creating Your Net Worth Statement

A *net worth statement* tells you how much you have after you add up your assets and subtract your liabilities. If for some odd reason you have to liquidate all your assets and pay off all your debts, what's left — your net worth — would be what you can take with you in a duffle bag into the woods.

The net worth statement isn't perfect: It'll be out of date tomorrow, as you continue to pay down your mortgage or increase your credit debt, but it can help you figure out whether you're financially stable or going broke. It can also give you peace of mind, assuming that your net worth is positive.

So how do you calculate your net worth? Let us explain.

Uncovering how much cash you've saved

When creating a net worth statement, start by adding your cash accounts. It's easy to figure out what you have: Open your bank's app and look at how much money you have in your savings and chequing accounts, and then add those numbers.

You might have other cash-based accounts, such as a high-interest savings account where you're socking away money for a new TV, or an emergency fund that you'd tap only if your roof caved in or your car broke down. Add those, too.

It's possible you may not know where all your cash is stashed. This situation is especially true if you had a spouse who managed the finances and has now passed away. In that case, look through any bank bills to see if you can locate the accounts you need. Or see if you can log into their account from their computer (passwords are often automatically saved) to try and figure out where those cash accounts reside.

Once you've added up all your cash, move onto your investments. Again, it's a lot easier to find out what's in an account today, though it may not be quite a simple as counting your loonies. Start by logging into your investment firm's website. The site could be a bank site, a secure page set up by your advisor, a mutual fund operation's client portal, or a robo-advisor's web page. Write down the value of your RRSP, TFSA, and any other investment accounts, including your pension, and then add those numbers.

Some people have accounts with different firms. If you know all the places where you've invested over the years, tallying up your savings is easy: Go to each site, find every account, and add the totals. (You can call your financial institutions as well if online banking or investing is not your thing.)

Over time, though, it can become difficult to remember where all your money is being kept. If you've changed jobs a few times but have continued to let your employers' pension company oversee your savings, you might have money with multiple firms. It's also possible to have more than one RRSP and TFSA. One way to refresh your memory is to take a few minutes to read through any financial documents or files you've received. You might have RRSP or TFSA statements that list the value of your assets or pension documents with asset totals. This information could come in handy if you can't easily access material online.

Evaluating your home

Don't get too excited the next time you see an article in the *Globe and Mail* proclaiming that your net worth is going up. The reporters aren't saying that you now have more cash to spend on your dream vacation. In all likelihood, they're referring to climbing real estate prices, which are a major contributor to a person's net worth.

Although you do include the value of your home in a net worth calculation, the value of your abode can make it seem as if you're rich when you're not. Unlike investments, which you can liquidate pretty much right away if need be, a house is a lot harder to sell quickly (well, except in Toronto and Vancouver, where people are chomping at the bit to buy high-priced homes).

Even if your house has climbed 50 percent over the last five years, hold off pretending you're Elon Musk. Still, real estate is an important part of a net worth calculation.

Here are a few ways to figure out the value of your home:

- Get your home appraised by a real estate agent. That person should know how much you could realistically get for your place.
- Search Realtor.ca (`www.realtor.ca`) for homes similar to yours and see how much they're listing for. (The listing price isn't as accurate as the selling price, but it will still give you a number you can use.)
- Search online for the average house price both in the year you bought your home and today. You can find this information on local real estate association websites; listing.ca (`https://listing.ca`) has the average home prices for several Ontario locales. Then calculate the percentage difference. Use that percentage to calculate how much your home is worth now. For instance, between 2015 and 2021, the average price of a detached home in Toronto climbed 78 percent, according to Listing.ca. So, if you bought your place for $900,000 in 2015, it would be worth about $1.6 million today.

Because a net worth statement captures a moment in time, don't work too hard to get these numbers; looking at Realtor.ca is usually good enough.

Including cars, jewellery, and art — or not

There are different schools of thought as to whether to add cars, jewellery, and art to a net worth statement.

Unless you have rare ride that might command a pretty penny, a car is a *depreciating asset*, which means it falls in value over time. However, you can still get something for that car, and depending on the model and year, it could be a sizable amount. We recommend adding a car to your net worth statement, in part because you need to also add what you owe for that vehicle. Use the current market value of the car — not what you paid for it. See your dealer to see how much you'd be paid if you decided to sell your car, or look it up on AutoTrader.ca (`www.autotrader.ca`).

What about jewellery? A lot of people calculate their net worth using liquid assets (or mostly liquid assets), which jewellery is not. It can be difficult to sell and hard to appraise, and its appraised price might not be what you can get for it when it comes time to sell. Jewellery also tends to get passed down from one generation to the next, so if you have no intention to ever sell it, don't include it.

The story is similar with art. Unless you're a major art collector, the pieces that adorn your walls are there because they look good, not because you bought them for an investment. The art you own will probably never sell. If you do manage to unload it, it'll most likely be at a garage sale, where you'll get a fraction of the original purchase price.

Divulging your debts

After you've added your assets, it's time to add your debts. Again, go to your bank or credit card company's website, where your credit card and line-of-credit debt should be displayed. Add those numbers together.

Next, if you own a home, find out how much you owe on your mortgage. Most lenders mail out a statement showing what you've paid and what you owe; you can also go to your lender's website.

If you pay rent, you won't need to worry about real estate in the net worth calculation. However, you'll include rent in the cash flow statement, which we touch on in the "It's All about the Cash Flow" section.

You might need to consider other debts, too. For example, annual taxes don't go on a net worth statement, but taxes you owe do. Overdue taxes are a liability. (If you owe taxes, pay up — you're accumulating interest every day, which makes the amount you owe rise even higher.)

Studying a sample net worth calculation

Calculating your net worth should be as easy as a grade 5 math test. If you have all your numbers at hand, you simply do some adding and subtracting. To figure out your net worth, just take your assets and subtract your liabilities:

assets – liabilities = net worth

That's it!

Here's an example of what a high net worth statement could look like, starting with a list of potential assets and liabilities:

Assets	Liabilities
Chequing account	Credit card debt
Savings account	Line-of-credit
Retirement account	Student loans
Pension	Mortgage debt
Other investments	Taxes
Real estate	Auto loans
Vehicles	Other debt

Now assign numbers to these categories. When calculating your net worth, change any categories as you see fit.

Assets	
Chequing account	$5,000
Savings account	$15,000
Retirement accounts (RRSP and TFSA)	$400,000
Pension	$100,000
Other investments accounts	$20,000
Real estate	$1,500,000
Vehicles	$30,000
Total	$2,070,000

Liabilities	
Credit card debt	$10,000
Line-of-credit	$5,000
Student loans	$2,000
Mortgage debt	$700,000
Auto loans	$15,000
Taxes	$3,000
Other debt	$10,000
Total	$745,000
Your net worth	***$1,333,000***

There you go! That's really all it takes to find out your net worth. You're in fairly good shape if the number is positive.

TIP: You can also try out one of the many online net worth statement calculators, such as the one at `www.cchwebsites.com/content/calculators/CANetWorth.html`.

There a few other things to consider when calculating your net worth, however:

- If you are getting a divorce and do not have a prenuptial agreement, assets are supposed to be split 50-50. So, if you have a joint bank account or have pooled your retirement savings, you might need to halve the total amounts.

- If you are getting a divorce and have a home, will you sell it and split the proceeds? Or will one spouse buy out the other? If you're the one who gets to keep the home, you can factor in the entire cost.
- As far as home prices are concerned, remember that a net worth statement is just a snapshot in time. If you plan to sell your home 20 years from now, in some ways the value of your home could be misleading. Yes, the average price of a house has climbed by 276.8 percent between 2000 and 2020, but our housing market could crash. Or it could triple in value. Before you call yourself a millionaire, just remember that real estate values can fluctuate.
- Your assets and the amount of money you invest will, we hope, grow over time. Of course, investments could tank, though historically the market has always climbed over the long term. Although a sizable portfolio might look good on a net worth statement, it's the amount you eventually sell those stocks for that matters most.

Don't panic if your net worth number is negative. You can increase your net worth, primarily by saving more and paying down debt. The more you can reduce your liabilities, the more you increase your net worth. Get the asset number higher and your total net worth figure will rise, too. It's a good idea to do this net worth calculation once a year to see if your net worth is rising or falling.

It's All about the Cash Flow

After you determine your net worth (by adding assets and subtracting liabilities), you should create a cash flow statement. In a *cash flow statement,* you add monthly income and subtract monthly expenses. This statement isn't a *budget,* which outlines what you're spending on specific items (though doing this work will make it easier to create a budget). Rather, a cash flow statement tells you whether you're spending more money than you're bringing in every month.

Why not create a cash flow statement before a net worth statement? A net worth statement gives you a big-picture view of your financial health, which is important for understanding where to go next. A cash flow statement, on the other hand, tells you more about your day-to-day finances. Are you making ends meet? Do you need to make adjustments now? How might a divorce or death affect your monthly spending?

As mentioned, the two parts of a cash flow statement are income and expenses, and that's what you learn about next.

Recording Sources of Income

People make money in many ways, but most of their dough comes in the form of a salary. Government payments, spousal support, and other kinds of income can also fatten up a bank account. In this section, you look at the key sources of income.

Sorting out your salary

Your biggest chunk of change comes from your workplace. When factoring in your income, you shouldn't just divide your annual salary by 12. You need to use after-tax income (your pay minus the stuff your employer deducts from your cheque, such as employment insurance and Canada pension plan contributions), so that you're calculating only the dollars you have access to every month. So look at your paycheque instead, which takes off taxes and other deductions. Do the same if you're hourly; see how much you make, on average, every month after deductions.

Don't include any bonuses, because they are often variable and tend to come only once a year.

Including your tiny savings account interest

Any money inside a savings account earns interest every month. You'll most likely leave it in the account to increase your savings, but that's money you're earning, which can be added to your cash flow statement. However, as we write this, savings accounts pay next to nothing. That situation might change as central banks start increasing their own lending rates (these overnight rates, as they're called, are tied into savings rates), but unless you have a lot of money sitting in a savings account, you're likely not earning much.

Noting dividend income

Many people hold dividend-paying stocks, which entitle shareholders to a percentage of a company's earnings. Dividend income is handled in two ways. It might be automatically reinvested into more shares of the company, in which case you don't include this income on a cash flow statement. However, some people take the dividends as a cheque or direct deposit in their bank account. (Plenty of older Canadians use dividend income to pay for day-to-day living.) In that case, you would include dividend income on your cash flow statement.

Tallying your pension income

It may seem as if pensions are only for auto workers or miners, but many people still pay into a workplace pension plan. Typically, you start withdrawing those funds when you decide to retire. If you receive a pension payment, include that income on your cash flow statement.

Transforming RRSP to RRIF income

Any Canadian who has an RRSP must turn it into a RRIF by age 72. (You can make that conversion as early as 55, but most people wait because you can't put money into a RRIF.)

Once you convert your account, you must withdraw a certain amount from it every year, based on a percentage of your total assets. Those withdrawals are income and should be added to your cash flow statement.

Counting your Canada pension plan

After you turn 18 and are working, you begin paying into the Canada pension plan (CPP). (That's partly why you were so shocked to see just how little money you were making.) When you turn 60, you can start getting some of that money back. What you earn depends on how long you've worked, your average annual earnings, and when you start withdrawing.

TIP: Wait until 70 to collect if you can because the payments will be larger than if you take CPP at 60. How so? Your payment decreases by 0.6 percent for every month you take CPP before 65 and increases by 0.7 percent for every month you wait to receive payments after 65. Say you were supposed to receive the CPP average of $619.75 per month at 65. If you start taking it at 60, you'll get only $396.64 per month. If you wait until you're 70, you'll get $880.04 per month.

CPP is paid monthly. If you're bereaved, you can collect part of your spouse's CPP too. What you receive depends on several factors, such as whether you're receiving other CPP benefits and your age. For more information, head to the Government of Canada's Survivor's Pension page at `www.canada.ca/en/services/benefits/publicpensions/cpp/cpp-survivor-pension.html`.

Logging old age security

Want free money? Look no further than old age security (OAS), a government pension given to Canadians 65 and older who have lived in Canada for at least 10 years since the age of 18. You can receive up to $642.25 per month, but if you earn $79,054 or more in other income, your OAS payment is smaller. Those who earn $128,149 or higher get nothing. (These two numbers are for 2022; the income at which payments start to decrease rises a bit every year.)

If you're bereaved and your income is less than $26,252, you might be able to receive part of your spouse's OAS.

Recording spousal support

If you're divorced, you might be entitled to spousal support, which typically comes in the form of a monthly payment. These payments usually go to the lower-earning spouse, who may not have had a chance to make as much, if anything, because they stayed home to take care of the children. An ex-spouse might also be entitled to support if they need extra financial support and the other person is financially able to help.

What you receive depends on several factors, such as the difference in income, if you and your ex had kids together, and your age. You'll need to talk to a lawyer to figure out what you can receive.

Calculating child support

A divorced person may also be entitled to child support, which is a monthly payment one parent makes to the other to help with costs associated with raising their kids. As with spousal support, the amount depends on both parents' income, where the kids will live, the cost of living, the province of residence, and more.

Remembering other income

Even with all the sources of income we've already discussed, you might still have others. The main one is likely rental income. Another source of income is a side hustle, which we talk about in Chapter 3. If you have a second home you're renting, whether it's an investment property or a seasonal cottage, any monthly income you make is considered income.

Expenses and Debt: The Necessary Evils

Calculating income is the fun part —who doesn't love to see how much money they're making? But to create a cash flow statement and to get an accurate look at your finances, you also need see how much money is leaving your bank account, including the amounts you're spending and how much you owe.

Let's get one thing out of the way: Debt is not inherently bad. If it weren't for debt, most people couldn't buy a house. Without a house, it's difficult to grow your net worth. Most people also couldn't afford a new car, but in many regions, you can't earn a living without access to a car. (We go much deeper into the topic of debt in Chapter 6.)

In this section, we go through some of the key expenses that you need to account for and include on a cash flow statement.

Rent or mortgage payments

Rent or mortgage payments will likely be your biggest monthly expense. And because both housing prices and rents are rising in Canada, these payments could be getting larger, too. The advantage of a mortgage is that it's possible to lower your monthly payments to better suit your cash flow needs.

You can refinance to pay over a longer period. Or if you have a variable-rate mortgage, you can potentially reduce your monthly payments if rates fall. (Although you might have to pay more if rates rise.) Mortgages can also eventually go to zero, while rents cannot. Add those monthly payments to a real estate expense line on the cash flow statement.

Credit card and line of credit debt

Credit card debt is the kind of debt you don't want, especially if you're using a rewards card that charges 20 percent interest, which most do. Line-of-credit debt usually comes with a lower interest rate, but it's still not a great idea to carry too much of it for too long.

If you can't pay off your debts every month, you'll have to fork over monthly payments, whether it's just the interest or interest plus principle. (Try for the latter.) Add those monthly payments to your expense line on your cash flow statement.

Utility, internet, cable and phone bills

You also need to include in your expenses all the monthly bills that make your house tick: electricity, gas, water, heating, and other housing bills. Also tally your internet, cable, and phone bills, as well as monthly subscription services, such as Netflix or Spotify. If you pay any of these yearly, divide the amount by 12 and use that monthly figure on your cash flow statement.

Groceries, restaurants, and entertainment

Most people pay about the same amount for groceries every month. They also often tend to spend about the same eating out and doing fun things on the weekend. You don't have to be exact for this cash flow exercise, so see how much you tend to spend in a month and insert that amount in your cash flow statement. (Read Chapter 4 for more on budgeting and food costs.)

Transportation

Unless you've bought your car outright, you're likely either paying off a car loan every month or leasing your vehicle. Both kinds of payments should be accounted for. At least car loan payments will eventually go to zero. If you take the bus or subway, factor in those monthly costs.

Insurance

You might have life, house or auto insurance payments. If you don't know the amounts — these things tend to get purchased and then forgotten about — you might need to look them up. After you have the amounts, add them to your expenses on your cash flow statement.

Property taxes and condo fees

If you own a home, you have to pay property taxes, which, in some provinces, can be paid monthly or annually. It's usually a good idea to pay property taxes monthly so you don't have to outlay a ton of cash. Any monthly condo fees should also be added to your cash flow calculation.

Spousal and child support

If you're receiving spousal or child support, it's income. If you're paying support, it's an expense. Both are usually paid every month, so you can easily factor them into your cash flow projections.

Savings

Why would savings go under expenses? Because even though you're not really spending this money, you want to make sure you have enough money every month to put a few bucks away into an investment account. So, consider savings an expense.

Calculating cash flow

After you've sorted out all the numbers, add up your income and then subtract the expenses. What's left over? If you're in the black, you'll have extra money to save, to use to pay down debt, or to allocate to another part of your budget (which, again, we'll get into in Chapter 4). If you're in the red, you'll need to find ways to reduce your spending or increase your income. The goal is to always be cash flow positive, whether you're single, divorced, or bereaved.

Saving Can Be Exciting!

The Oracle of Omaha, billionaire investor Warren Buffett, once said: "Do not save what is left after spending, but spend what is left after saving." If only it were that easy, but the sentiment is spot on. The only way to get financially ahead in life is to pay yourself first.

Saving money — and paying down debt — isn't just good for your bank account; it's good for your psyche. According to the Harvard Business Review, which surveyed more than 12,000 people who had applied for loans to eliminate their credit card debt, those who had at least $500 cash on hand reported a 15 percent higher life satisfaction than those who did not.

An older study from Ally Bank found that among those with savings accounts, 38 percent reported feeling extremely or very happy compared to 29 percent of people without a savings account. The same study also found that the more money people saved, the happier they were. Of those who said they were extremely or very happy, 57 percent had at least $100,000 in savings, 42 percent had between $20,000 and $100,000, and

34 percent had less than $20,000. Finally, Ally Bank found that 84 percent of people said saving money boosted their sense of well-being more than eating healthy food, having a good job, or getting regular exercise.

It also helps to earn more money. There has been a long-held belief that more money after reaching the $75,000 mark doesn't make people happier. However, studies conducted in 2020 (`https://psycnet.apa.org/record/2020-43605-001`) and in 2021 (`www.pnas.org/doi/10.1073/pnas.2016976118`) found that more money does indeed buy more happiness. Still, trying to earn more isn't the holy grail here. Growing savings, which can be done whether you make $50,000 or $150,000 a year, is the key to building a happier life.

Keep the fact that saving matters most in mind as you embark on or continue your single journey. If you are feeling overwhelmed or your finances aren't lining up the way you'd like, take a breath, regroup, talk to a professional, and come up with a solid savings plan. You'll begin feeling better after you start seeing your savings account (or investment account) balance rise.

It's important to start saving now — the earlier you get going, the better off you'll be. For instance, suppose you put $50,000 in an investment account at age 25 and add $10,000 a year to that account. If those funds grow at a 5 percent annual rate of return, you'll have about $1.6 million in your investment account by the time you turn 65. If you do the same at 40, you'll have made $670,450 by retirement age. Start at 50 and you'll have $330,521 at 65.

Looking Ahead to Retirement

There are plenty of reasons for saving. Splurging on a big night out, a fancy picture frame television, a week-long trip to Maui, a child's education — the list goes on. Almost everyone needs to put at least some money away for their golden years, when they may no longer be earning a consistent income, if they earn one at all.

Despite all the bank commercials showing gray-haired couples frolicking together in retirement, you can have a perfectly happy post-working life on your own. You might, however, need to put a little more money away, given that the single life costs more.

Saving for retirement is trickier if the plans you made with a spouse get thrown out the window in a divorce, but a split doesn't spell the end of your retirement goals. You just need to save more to afford the Mexican villa you had your sights set on. Or you might need to shift your goals. (Maybe you hated the idea of the villa! Now's your chance to find something that suits you better.)

Contrary to what many financial institutions would have you believe, saving for retirement might not be as difficult as you think. If you have a workplace pension that you're automatically putting money into every paycheque, you might already have a sizable nest egg built up. CPP and OAS can also add to your retirement income. If your spouse passes away, you can put life insurance money, which is not taxed, into your RRSP or TFSA. In addition, expenses tend to decline in your later years: If you're lucky, there will be no more kids to pay for (fingers crossed!) and no more mortgage to pay down.

TIP

What's most important is to start thinking about retirement now. Yes, you need to start saving right away, but you need to think about more than just money. Give some thought to what you want to do, who you want to spend your retirement with, the hobbies and activities that make you happy, and what kind of healthcare needs you might need. Then figure out how much it will cost to do all of that and more.

3

Facing Your Financial Future

You've completed your net worth and cash flow statements, so it's time to take control of your financial life. Whether you already have a good paying job or need to find one after staying home for years to look after the children, living off one income is different than living off two. You can't rely on anyone else to support, or further enhance, your day-to-day lifestyle. And the goals you set when you were younger, either as a single 20-something or as part of a couple, will need to adapt and evolve to your current situation.

Now it's time to do the hard work: finding a financial advisor, investing for your future goals, and potentially earning additional income.

Exploring Ways to Allocate Your Money

There's safety in numbers. When you're coupled up, you can take a leave of absence from your day job, stay home to take care of the children, or get laid off, all without worrying that your household income will go to zero.

Thankfully, it's a lot easier to earn money these days, especially after the pandemic, because you can now work remotely. On the flipside, it can also be a lot easier to spend money when you're on your own. There's no one to gut-check an expense, and takeout dinner is a press of an app away. You also might feel the need to pamper yourself with a weekly spa day or a regular night out for drinks.

Keeping your saving and spending in check requires that you create a budget, but before we get there in Chapter 4, you should think about how you're going to pay for your life.

Where can you start? Here are a few ways to ensure that you have enough cash to keep going.

Creating an airtight budget

Most people would rather do just about anything than create a budget, but you're going to need one to ensure that you can pay for your expenses. Fortunately, making a budget is not difficult. Set aside a few hours on a Sunday to go through your debit and credit card statements and add up your monthly income and expenses. You'll have already done a lot of this work if you created a cash flow statement (see Chapter 2), but you may need to find a few more items for this exercise. We get into more detail on how to create a budget in Chapter 4.

Allocating money to more than one bank account

The last thing you want is to spend the money you need to live on. One way to prevent that from happening is to keep your day-to-day money separate from your *discretionary dollars,* funds that you might use for your wants rather than needs.

Consider creating two bank accounts: one that holds cash for groceries, utilities, mortgage payments, and so on and the other for your fun money for travel, concerts, restaurants, and bigger purchases.

It's easier to allocate your funds after you create a budget, but you can also use the *80/20 rule,* which says to put 80 percent of your money in the daily account and 20 percent in the fun account. The point is to make sure you don't accidently spend your milk money on cocktails.

Following the 70/20/10 rule

Many savings rules are available, but here's a common one that many people use and like. First, take 70 percent of your monthly paycheque and put it towards your monthly expenses. Then take 20 percent of your monthly salary and add it to your investments. Finally, use the remaining 10 percent to pay down any debt. This approach isn't perfect — for example, sometimes you can earn more by paying down debt than by investing (see Chapter 7) — but it's a start.

Understanding the three-bucket strategy

Retirees sometimes use the *three-bucket strategy,* where they split your money into three buckets: short term, intermediate, and long term. Invest your long-term funds into higher growth assets. Take the profits and dividends from those investments and put them into medium-term securities, such as bonds or stable dividend paying stocks. Put the income earned from those assets into the final bucket, which is an account to fund your day-to-day expenses.

The three-bucket strategy could take some time to establish depending on how much you have invested, and it's risky, especially if markets decline and you lose money. But if you can set it up correctly, your money will start working for you instead of the other way around.

TIP Before implementing any strategy into your portfolio, be informed, ask the experts, and then ensure that it's a fit for you and your goals.

Boosting Your Income

Saving and investing aren't the only ways to improve your financial health: Earning more income is a grand idea too. If you've been out of the workforce a few years, perhaps taking care of the children or an elderly parent, you might need to find employment. (Spousal support, which we get into in Chapter 6, can help keep dollars coming in.)

Even if you already have a job, you might want to find ways to increase your income. Perhaps you want to buy a new house for yourself and your kids. Or maybe, after all you've been through, you want to treat yourself to a luxurious vacation. Fortunately, making money is, in some ways, easier than ever before.

Taking advantage of passive income

Who wouldn't love to make money while they're sleeping? That's the idea behind *passive income,* which is cash you earn while you're doing something else. Fortunately, you don't have to be the CEO of a multimillion technology firm to make money doing nothing. Here are a few ways to produce more than a few pennies passively:

- **Invest in dividend-paying securities.** One tried-and-true way of earning a passive income is through dividend-paying stocks. Dividend-paying companies pay out a percentage of their earnings to their shareholders quarterly or annually. Every dividend-paying company pays something different, but the payout is based also on the share price of the business and how many shares you own. Here's how dividend payments works: If company X pays a 4 percent dividend yield and you own 10,000 shares that trade at $100 per share, you'll earn $400 on those shares every year. A lot of people reinvest that money into more shares, but you can take it as cash and use it to fund your expenses.
- **Airbnb your abode.** Have you ever wanted to be a hotelier? With Airbnb, you can not only play the role of a good hotel host but also earn some money doing it. Millions of people around the world have turned their primary and secondary residences into passive-income-generating machines. According to low-interest lender Earnest, Airbnb hosts earn $924 a month on average. If you've got a dashing dwelling, why not give this a shot? Also check out Turo, which is the Airbnb for cars.

- **Rent out real estate the old-fashioned way.** You don't have to use Airbnb to rent real estate. If you have a cottage that you never use — maybe you got it in a divorce or don't need it now that your spouse has passed away — rent it for the summer or, if it's winterized, the entire year. Post the rental on your local community Facebook group and you'll find a renter in no time.
- **Start a YouTube channel.** There's money to be made online. Maybe you can be the champion for single people everywhere, or perhaps you have some other talent you haven't shared with the world. Although you'll never make as much as Ryan Kaji, the 8-year-old who brings in $26 million a year playing with toys and doing other kid stuff, you can earn between $3 and $5 for every 1,000 views.

Working a side hustle for profit and fun

Unless you own a lot of rental-ready real estate or have a dividend portfolio, you're not going to make a boatload from passive income. Have no fear, work is here! These days, there are plenty of ways to earn money outside your nine-to-five-day job. According to Abacus data, 31 percent of Canadians have a side hustle. And website Side Hustle Nation says that the average side gig brings in $1,122 month.

A side hustle could be ideal for singles who have more time on their hands at night, want to add a little extra income to supplement their spousal support, or would like to keep busy now that their partner has passed away.

If you're going to start a side hustle, make sure it's something you enjoy. Turn a hobby into a money-making venture, work on your big business idea, sell something you know others will love. Here are some ideas:

- **Start a wholesale business.** Buy low, sell high. That's essentially the idea with warehousing: You buy something in bulk at a discounted rate and then sell each individual item at the regular retail price. You'll need to front some cash to make this work, but if what you're selling is in high demand, it's possible to make a pretty penny.
- **Open an e-commerce store.** There's a market for almost anything these days — even the stuff you make when you're bored at night. If you have a craft that you love to create, why not sell it to the masses? It's never been easier to launch an online store. You can set one up in minutes through Shopify (`www.shopify.com`) or Etsy (`www.etsy.com`).
- **Be around what you love.** Do you have a passion for golfing? Working out? Fashion? Consider finding a part-time job at your local club, gym, or retailer. Plenty of places would jump at the chance to hire someone

who is passionate about what they do and isn't going to quit when something better comes along. Bonus: You could get benefits at these jobs that will save you more money, such as free golfing, a complimentary gym membership, or an employee discount at the store.

Planning Your Dream Life by Setting Financial Goals

There's not a traveller out there who doesn't need some sort of map to help them see where they're going. You might have replaced the paper map that you used to spread out on the dashboard prior to a road trip with Waze or Google Maps, but you're still using something to guide you. It's the same thing with money — how can you know how much you should save or invest without a of plan?

A lot of people have trouble coming up with financial goals, especially if they're in their 30s and 40s with so much of their life still ahead of them. How can you possibly know what you want to do in retirement or how much anything might cost 30 years from now? That thinking, however, will prevent you from doing anything at all. It's also not accurate. You can approximate how much you'll need in retirement. And if you think carefully, you can probably figure out a few things to do in your golden years.

Don't worry; goals can evolve. What you might want to do in your 30s isn't necessarily what you will do in your 60s. This is especially true for singles who had either planned on being part of a twosome and for those who are divorced or bereaved. For the former, you might have to rethink how you plan on living in retirement, though you might not have to adjust your plans substantially. If you had dreamed of travelling the world with a significant other, you can probably still do that with a later-in-life partner, a close friend, or a group of retirees.

If you're divorced or bereaved, you'll probably have to adjust your goals in more significant ways. You and your partner may have had a dream retirement that's no longer going to happen. Adjusting those plans may be more emotional than anything else — it can be difficult to imagine yourself doing something differently than you had always envisioned — but once you come around to some new ideas, financial planning for them doesn't have to be a challenge.

You'll want to save for two kinds of goals: *short-term goals,* which are those things you want to do now and over the next few years, and *long-term goals,* such as retirement and other major life activities you want to accomplish over the next 15 to 30 years.

Here are some short-term goals you might have:

- Travel
- Renovations
- Milestone birthday party

- New car
- Big ticket item you've always wanted
- Children's education

And these are more long-term goals:

- Travel
- Spending time with friends or family
- Furthering your education
- Vacation or retirement property
- Funding healthcare needs
- More golf, tennis, and pickleball

If you take a minute, you can probably come up with a good list of goals to start saving for. Why don't you do that right now? We don't mind waiting.

Saving for short-term goals

Now that you've figured out your short-term and long-term goals (we assume that you planned out your entire life while we were patiently waiting for you to return), it's time to price them. Let's start with short-term goals. Want to go to Fiji in three years? Look at how much flights, hotels, a few excursions, and the average meal might cost and add it up. (You might find a travel package that combines hotel, flights, food, and day trips.) Sure, prices can change, so add a few extra hundred bucks to give yourself some cushion. Do the same for the car, the birthday party, or your child's university education.

The hardest part of this process is not the internet searching but saving for your goals. With a little discipline, though, you should be able to put at least something away. Here are some ways to save for more immediate plans:

- **Automatically move money to savings.** As we said previously, the key to saving is to pay yourself first. Before you buy anything, put whatever you must save into a savings account.

  TIP: The most efficient way to do this is to have your bank automatically move part of each paycheque — say on the 1st and 15th of the month — into your savings. Not only do you not have to remember to move the money yourself, but this option will prevent you from spending it, too.

- **Every month, allocate a set amount to each goal.** Saying you'll put $2,000 into your travel fund in two months rarely works. Instead, divide the amount to reach the goal by the number of months it will take to save enough money. Say the trip you want to go on in 5 years costs $20,000. If you divide that amount by 60 months, you'll see that you need to save $333 every month. Once you hit 5 years, stop saving and go spend those dollars. (Bonus: A smaller monthly number feels more manageable that a larger yearly one.)

- **Set up more than one savings account.** A lot of people think that they can have only one savings account and one chequing account, but that's not true. You can have as many savings accounts as you'd like (though you might have to pay bank fees on each). If you have multiple goals you want to save for, set up a few savings accounts and put money away in each one every month. After you've used the money, you can either close that account or use it to save for your next goal.
- **Put money in guaranteed investment certificates (GICs).** If you want to earn a little interest on your savings and you don't plan on using that money before you need it, consider stashing your funds in a GIC. These investment securities are a cross between a bank account and a bond. Like a bank account, you can't lose any money by putting your money into one. Similar to a bond, you get paid interest for loaning your cash to your financial institution for a set amount of time, typically between 6 months and 5 years. However, if you need to remove money from a GIC, you could be hit with a hefty fee. With rates so low right now, make sure that what you're getting paid to lock in is worth it.

- **Use a savings app.** We get into budgeting apps in the next chapter, but a lot those same apps come with goal-budgeting features. These programs let you choose goals and set targets, and many can be synced to your bank account. Strides (`www.stridesapp.com`) is a popular goal-savings programs — check it out in your favourite app store.

Investing for long-term goals

A note of caution: Don't put your short-term money into any investments that could decline in value in any significant way. If you need $30,000 in 3 years for a new car, do not put those dollars in stocks, which can drop in price at any moment. Instead, keep that money in cash or put it into a guaranteed investment certificate, which pays interest, but doesn't decline in value. However, investing is ideal for any goals 10 to 30 years from now because, historically, markets always go up if given enough time.

Conceptually, putting money away for your long-term needs isn't that different from your short-term ones. The best way to save for retirement, for instance, is to automatically take money out of every paycheque and put it into an investment account. You still need to price out your goals — figuring out how much retirement might cost will take more work than looking up the cost of a TV online, but it's the same idea. Where long-term goals differ is in how you'll grow your money. Putting cash into a savings account every month isn't enough — you need to get help from the market, too.

It's likely that most of your long-term savings will go into either a TFSA or an RRSP, both of which we describe later in this chapter. For now, we talk about the kinds of investment instruments you may need to purchase to help fund your future.

Investing in stocks

A *stock* gives you a share in a company. While most shareholders get the right to vote on various company matters, such as executive compensation and the directors of the board, people tend to own stocks because they have the potential to rise in value, thus expanding their wealth. The value of a share can rise or fall for many reasons, but basically, if a company's earnings go up year after year, so too will the price of that stock.

You can choose from all kinds of companies, depending on how much risk you want to take. Fast-growing tech companies can potentially help you grow your nest egg more rapidly than a boring bank, but if something goes awry, it could fall harder than a kid after a sugar high.

You must invest in stocks to meet your long-term goals, but what to invest in is different for every individual. Some people want to choose individual stocks, something you can learn more about in *Stock Picking For Canadians for Dummies* (Wiley), but the average person should consider buying equity mutual funds and exchange-traded funds (ETFs), which we talk more about later in the chapter.

Investing in bonds

Bonds are the other big investment that most people know about. Governments and companies issue *bonds* when they want to raise money. Bonds are typically issued to fund a specific project, to fund general growth, to pay down debt, and more. When you buy the bond, you're loaning money to the *issuer* — that's the company or government — in exchange for a regular payment, which is typically distributed monthly, quarterly, or annually.

Bonds come with a *term,* which is usually 6 months to 5 years, although some can range between 10 to 30 years. If you hang on to that security for the entire time, you'll get back all the money you originally put into it, which is why bonds are consider safer than stocks. Unless the government or company runs into major financial trouble and can't pay interest, you'll make your money back and then some thanks to the regular distributions. However, bonds aren't foolproof and many companies and even some governments have defaulted on their loans.

As with stocks, the riskier the asset — and therefore the more potential it has to go bust — the more you'll make in interest. As well, a 30-year bond pays more than a 5-year bond because there's more potential for the issuer to run into trouble over three decades rather than 60 months.

It's hard for the average person to buy single bonds themselves, which means they usually have to purchase a bond mutual fund or exchange-traded fund to get into this market. These funds are subject to some ups and downs because managers tend to trade bonds rather than just hold onto them for decades until they can collect the principal. Still, bonds are less volatile than stocks, meaning they don't rise or fall nearly as much as the broader market. In fact, when certain stocks correct, certain bonds can do well because investors tend to remove their money from risky assets to invest in safer ones. Depending on your financial situation, bonds may be a good instrument in your portfolio to balance out the volatility of your other holdings.

Investing in mutual funds and exchange-traded funds

There's a good chance your portfolio already has some mutual funds and exchange-traded funds (ETFs) because they hold stocks, bonds, and various other financial instruments within them. Mutual funds and ETFs are similar in that they both hold a variety of stocks or bonds in one investment. However, ETFs can be cheaper to hold than mutual funds because these securities follow a predetermined index. You don't have to pay a fund manager to pick stocks like you do with a mutual fund. ETFs also trade like a stock on an exchange. (For more on ETFs, see Bryan's *ETFs For Canadians For Dummies.*)

One benefit of a mutual fund is that it's already diversified. You don't have to choose any of the stocks, and you don't have to worry if one company in the fund goes bust because the others are there to keep things afloat. You can choose from thousands of funds, but for any investing, consider getting the assistance of a trusted professional to help guide you in the direction that works best for your financial goals.

What funds you choose will depend on your risk tolerance and time horizon. Remember, the general rule is that stocks are more volatile than bonds and therefore capable of a greater return. The classic balanced portfolio, for reference, is 60 percent stocks and 40 percent bonds.

As for time horizon, as people get closer to retirement, they become more conservative with their investments (meaning they increase the less volatile portion of their portfolio, therefore decreasing their overall risk). The reason? The closer you get to needing that money, the less you want to subject it to market's ups and downs. This thinking is still useful, but it's not as black and white as it used to be. If you already have a lot saved and then receive a large insurance payment, in the case of a spouse or partner passing away, you might not need all that cash in retirement. In that case, you may want to keep what you do need in more conservative investments and put the rest, depending on your goals, in longer-term options.

TIP

Whatever you do, investing for the long term requires putting money away consistently. Whether you do so every paycheque, every year, or somewhere in between, the key is to prioritize your savings.

Choosing a Financial Advisor

You might have a handle on how to live life alone, but when it comes to your finances, it helps to find a partner. We're talking about a financial advisor who can help you make smart investing and saving decisions based on your personal financial goals. Advisors can be especially helpful after a divorce or a death, when you're in a highly emotional state and need to get your affairs in order. Some people don't think they need professional help, but we think otherwise.

Understanding the financial advisor's role

Financial advisors have historically had one job: to invest your money. While there are still many advisors who care only about investing, the profession has changed a lot over the last few years. Good advisors not only manage your dough but also understand the many nuances of your life. They know that the only way to calm you can calm yourself down after a fight with your ex is to go on a shopping spree. They're well aware of the problems your oldest kids are having finding a job and how you have to support them in tough times. They want to make sure you get that much needed vacation. They're a therapist, a friend, and a money maven — the financial partner in your life.

More practically, a financial advisor can help you:

- Budget
- Devise a financial plan that fits your needs
- Choose the right investments
- Create passive income streams
- Prepare for tax time
- Review divorce settlements for financial issues
- Help claim life insurance benefits
- Ensure that you're leaving enough to your children
- Design a charitable giving plan
- Gain peace of mind

If you're still not sold on working with an advisor, think of it this way: If your car broke down, would you fix it yourself or take it to a mechanic? You would very likely do the latter. And if you do decide to tinker on your own, don't be surprised if your ride stops running in the middle of the highway. The same is true with a financial advisor.

Choosing an advisor for your situation

A lot of people have a financial advisor, but many find that person when they're already coupled up. Then after a major life change such as a divorce or a death, they want to deal with someone else. You should work with someone who has your back and with whom you feel comfortable. And although some financial advisors have expertise in divorce and death (certified divorce financial analysts, for instance), you don't need someone with that designation. Pretty much all advisors have clients who have dealt with every possible life event.

Finding the right advisor

Canada has more than 90,000 financial advisors, which means plenty of capable professionals can help you sort out your financial life. But there are also a lot of folks who you wouldn't want near your hard-earned dollars.

Finding the right advisor to work with is not an exact science — there's no one person who is the best at managing your money. Instead, find someone who suits your particular needs. Here's are two key things you'll want in an advisor:

- **Alignment:** An advisor must understand you and your life's goals. If everything goes well, you could be working together for decades. You need to be sure that the advisor will care about your wants and needs and help you get through difficult times, both emotionally and financially. In addition, the way the advisor approaches investing and saving must align with yours. For instance, if you want to own ETFs but the advisor doesn't like them, don't use that advisor.

- **Approachability:** While your advisor doesn't need to be your best friend, you have to feel comfortable coming to that person when the going gets tough. Money is wrapped up in all we do — losing a job, asking for custody of the kids, and falling in love again will have an effect on your financial wellbeing. You need to feel okay calling up your advisor and talking to them about challenging or embarrassing things.

Finding the right advisor

Trying to find a financial advisor can be overwhelming. There are so many and they often have similar qualifications and backgrounds. But given how important this relationship could become, you don't want to go with the first person you see online.

As with any service, the best way to find out about someone is through word of mouth. So, first ask around to see who your friends, family, and acquaintances use to help them manage their finances. Get three to five names and then look them up to find out a little more about who they are and what they do. Here are a few things to look for when doing your research:

- **Do they have a CFP designation?** The certified financial planner certification is a popular designation among advisors. To get it, advisors must take the required education, pass a few challenging exams, present a case study, and then take a minimum of 25 hours of continuing education classes every year. (Julie got her CFP designation in 2010 and is happy she doesn't have to take that exam again!) Most importantly, they have to adhere to a code of ethics which mandates putting their clients' interests first.

TIP Always work with someone who has CFP next to their name.

- **Do they live nearby?** When video chatting is the norm, it doesn't matter where your advisor lives. However, there's something to be said for being able to meet your advisor in the flesh when needed. Maybe you have a financial emergency and want to talk face-to-face, or you want to look your advisor in the eyes to see how the person is reacting to a 40 percent market decline. It's also nice to get taken out for a drink once in a while.
- **Are they registered with IIROC or MFDA?** The Investment Industry Regulatory Organization of Canada (IIROC) and Mutual Fund Dealers Association (MFDA) of Canada are the two self-regulatory organizations that oversee the investment industry in Canada. The big

difference between the two is that IIROC advisors can sell any kind of security, including stocks and ETFs, but MFDA advisors can sell only mutual funds.

These days, you want access to every kind of investment, even if you may not use it, so consider choosing an IIROC licensed advisor.

- **Have they ever been in trouble?** Before you meet with potential advisors, vet them first by seeing if any disciplinary action has been lodged against them. An internet search on their name is a good place to start, but you'll also want to go to search on their regulators' website, either or `www.mfda.ca`. For instance, when Bryan looks up Julie's name on the IIROC website to see if any disciplinary cases have been brought against her or if she has any unpaid fines, nothing comes up. (Thankfully, or an awkward conversation would be happening just now.) The Canadian Securities Administrators also has a national registration search that can tell you if the advisor you're considering is indeed licensed to sell securities in Canada. (Julie checks out there, too!)

After you know that a potential advisor is legit, you can start setting up meetings to see which one is best for you. You should ask that person a series of questions in your interview:

- **Why are you an advisor?** It's a good idea to find out what makes the advisor tick. What parts of the profession are they most passionate about? What drives them? What motivated them to get into this business? Was it to help others? To make a lot of cash?
- **What's your educational background and how are you continuing to educate yourself today?** While your advisor doesn't have to be an Ivy League grad, they should have some financial education. It can help to have a business degree, and maybe you want that person to be an economics major because you know nothing about how supply and demand might affect your investments. Plenty of advisors get into the business later in life, maybe after seeing how much people in their previous industry struggled with their money. That's fine, as long as their background fits with your needs.

  Also, ask them about their designations and what kinds of courses they're taking now. You want to make sure the person you're dealing with is committed to the profession and won't disappear after six months.
- **How do you get paid?** This is a big question and one you should not feel weird about asking. Traditionally, advisors were paid either by mutual fund companies for selling their funds (despite the advisor not being

employed by that company) or by commissions on a per-trade basis. Many still get paid in one of those ways, but it can give rise to a conflict of interest. How can you be sure that the investments the advisor is making are in your best interest?

Many advisors are moving away from this type of compensation and towards a fee-for-service model. This can work in a few ways: You might be charged a flat rate for a specific offering, a set hourly rate for ongoing work, or a fee based on the assets the advisor manages. So, as a rough example, if you have $500,000 in your portfolio and your advisor charges you a 1 percent fee on your assets, you'll owe them $5000 for the year. The advisor might spread their fee out over every month.

- **What services do you provide?** For many years, most advisors did one thing: investing. That was it — no budgeting, no financial planning, no hand-holding. Times have changed, but there are still a lot of advisors who want only to oversee investments. The best planners, however, do much more than that. They can help you create a budget, develop goals, get through a life insurance claims process, purchase life insurance, build a proper estate plan, and more. They should also have a network of other professionals they can refer you to, such as lawyers, accountants, bankers, and mortgage brokers, so that your entire financial life is accounted for. (By the way, you can, and should, ask these same questions of any service professional.)

- **How will our relationship work?** There was once a time not long ago when advisors and clients would meet once a year. Many still do, but the touch points have increased, whether through newsletters, video chats, or phone calls. For some people, a once-a-year meeting is fine, but others may want to talk to their advisor once a month. Ask potential advisors how often they meet, how they communicate with their clients, how you can contact them if you're feeling uneasy about your finances, and so on. If you prefer more contact, don't go with someone who likes to reach out only in December.

Determining what you can afford

We explained the main ways advisors get paid in the preceding section, but which way is right for you? It depends, in part, on your budget and what you want from the advisor. You don't have to invest your money with a professional — you can do it on your own, which we talk about next. But you may want to get help creating a financial plan. Advisors often charge between $3,000 and $5,000 for such a plan.

If the advisor is investing for you, your fee will likely be between 0.5 percent and 2 percent, depending on how much money they're managing. Usually, the advisor will simply debit money from your account to pay themselves according to your agreement, or use cash in the account or free up cash by selling investments. In that case, you don't have to outlay any additional money because they're taking payment from what's already there. You could also ask them to bill you so that you can pay them using money that's not in the account.

What's best? Paying out of pocket is ideal because you can keep the money in your portfolio invested in the market. You should speak with any potential advisor about what makes the most sense for your tax and financial situation.

Choosing between a human advisor and a robo-advisor

The rise of the robos, the robo-advisor revolution, the robot resurgence: These are just some of the ways that people have described the increasingly popular do-it-yourself robo-advisor investing platform. A *robo-advisor* is an online platform that, for the most part, does your investing for you. You transfer money from your bank account to the robo-advisor and those assets are divided into a variety of diversified ETFs according to your profile. Most robo-advisors come with a slick app and web interface that makes it easy to see how much you've lost or gained.

Online investing isn't new — Canadians have had the ability to pick stocks and funds via web-based discount brokerages since the 1990s — but do-it-yourself investing usually requires you to choose stocks yourself. Robo-advisors have already selected the funds they'll put your money into; you simply put cash into the desired account (for example, an RRSP or TFSA) and away you go.

Note that the name *robo-advisor* is misleading because most of these sites don't offer advice. While some Canadian banks do provide robo-advisor platforms that can be used alongside a bank advisor, their platforms are still geared toward do-it-yourself (DIY) investors. This is partly why there's been a rise in fee-only planners; robo-advisors make it easy for anyone to invest for themselves online, but you still need the financial planning advice that only a human can provide. In fact, a lot of advisors are now using robo-advisors to manage their clients' investments, allowing them to spend less time concentrating on markets and more time helping their clients achieve their financial goals.

There are a lot of good reasons to use a robo, including the fact that they're fairly inexpensive compared to owning a portfolio of mutual funds. Depending on how much you invest, you may have pay only about 0.5 percent of your total assets on an annual basis.

The other big advantage is that the portfolios automatically rebalance so that your allocation of stocks and bonds is always as it should be. This feature is important because if the market does really well and you don't rebalance, your target portfolio of 60 percent stocks and 40 percent bonds could end up being invested in more stocks than you want based on your risk tolerance level. When that allocation gets too out of whack, the robo automatically sells stock and buys bonds to get those numbers back in balance. The opposite is also true when the market falls — you could end up with a lower exposure to equities than you'd like. Before robos, investors had to rely on their advisors to rebalance (or do it themselves if they were DIY investors).

Robos suit a variety of investor profiles and can be an ideal solution for busy singles who may not have the time to invest on their own and don't feel as though they need an advisor to invest on their behalf. If that sounds like you, you'll want to do some research on the many robos available. Start with MoneySense's *Guide to the Best Robo Advisors in Canada,* which Bryan helped write.

As good as robos are, humans still have plenty of value, too. For one, robos tend to invest in a basic suite of ETFs. Humans can create a more nuanced portfolio that might better suit your needs. To make the comparison a little easier, we created this handy chart to show you how robos and humans stack up:

	Robos	Humans
Invest for you	Yes	Yes
Personalized investing	Not usually	Yes
Automated investing	Yes	No
Financial advice	No	Yes
Rebalance automatically	Yes	Usually
Tax, insurance, and estate planning	No	Yes
Easy-to-understand interface	Yes	Not often
Cost efficient	Yes	Not always
Emotional management	No	Yes
Meet with you for coffee	No	Yes

TIP

As you can see, robos are geared towards investing, while humans can tackle all aspects of financial advice.

Vetting the best person or online platform

Deciding whether to use a robo-advisor or a person comes down to whether or not you also need financial advice. Given that robos do all the investing, you don't need to be a savvy stock picker like you would if you were a DIY investor using an online brokerage firm. A lot of people now use a combination of an online platform for investing and a person for advice.

So how can you decide what's best? Here are a few questions to ask yourself.

- **Do you need financial advice?** This is the main question to consider. If you're newly divorced or widowed, the answer could very well be yes. You'll probably need some help figuring out where to put recently divided assets or a life insurance lump sum, the best way to pay down debts, how to properly budget for a single person, and more. If you need this kind of help, to with a human.
- **Do you need investing advice?** As easy as it is to invest with a robo-advisor, there are limitations. Most divide your assets across a few ETFs. They do ask you a few questions to determine your risk tolerance level, which is then used when allocating stocks versus bonds, but that's about as involved as it gets. What if you want more technology stocks than what the robo offers or a greater exposure to U.S. stocks versus Canadian ones? In these cases, call an advisor who can create a more personalized portfolio.
- **How much are you willing to spend?** As we said, robos can be cheaper to use than a human. If you don't need advice and are fine with what the robos are investing your money in, their prices are hard to beat. If you need more services, make sure that you're getting good value for what you're paying the advisor.

A reasonable fee is 1 percent to 2.5 percent of your total assets on an annual basis. The more you pay, the more services or options you should get, whether it's from an advisor or a robo.

Comparing robos

Although most robos have the same basic purpose — to make investing easier and more understandable for the average person — they're all a little different. Some give you more investing options, some offer access to insurance products, and some have better interfaces than others.

Following are the top Canadian robo advisors and their fees:

Robo advisor	Fee
BMO Smartfolio	0.4% to 0.7%
CI Direct Investing	0.35% to 0.6%
iA WealthAssist	0.7%
Justwealth	0.4% to 0.5% or $4.99 a month for accounts with less than $12,000
Nest Wealth	$5 to $150 a month
Questwealth	0.2% to 0.25%
RBC InvestEase	0.5%
Smart Money Invest	0.8%
VirtualWealth	0.35% to 0.6%
Wealthsimple	0.4% to 0.5%

Do an internet search on each one and also visit `www.moneysense.ca/save/investing/best-robo-advisors-in-canada/` to find out what each company offers.

Calling It a Career: Knowing When You Should Retire

Once upon a time, most Canadian workers strove for Freedom 55 — or at least Freedom 65. (Freedom 55, by the way, is a Winnipeg-based financial company, but their commercials became synonymous with retirement, like how people say "Kleenex" when they just want a tissue.) While many people still retire in their 50s and 60s, more people are also working well into their 70s and 80s. Others are spending half their time working and half vacationing, while a lot of older people are starting businesses, going back to school, or embarking on second careers. As you can see, there are no longer rules around retirement.

People are charting their own retirement paths instead of calling it a career at 65 for several reasons. For one, pensions have changed. The Greatest Generation — those born in the 1900s to 1920s — worked blue collar jobs and had a *defined benefit (DB)* pension, which essentially guaranteed a set payment for life upon retirement. After you were eligible to start receiving payments, you said goodbye to your workplace. Now, most companies have shifted to a *defined contribution (DC)* plan, which requires employees to fund most of the account, though employers often match contributions. The value of a DC rises and falls over time. Because the onus to pay into the pension is now on the employee, many choose not to invest. Plus, many people work for companies that don't offer a pension plan.

At the same time, people are living longer and don't want to spend 20 years of their lives not doing anything. And the way we work has changed, too. You can work from anywhere and can more easily pick up part-time jobs (as described in the "Working a side hustle for profit and fun" section), which makes partial retirement easier to do.

When deciding whether to call it quits, ask yourself the following:

- **Do you want to keep working?** If you still love the 9 to 5, why stop? You could try something different or work part time, but don't stop if you don't want to.
- **Have you saved enough?** A lot of people continue to work because they need to keep earning a living. If you have enough money to get you through your 90s — most advisors now use 95 as the date they plan against — feel free to call it quits.

- **Have you met your financial goals?** You may have enough money to stop working, but do you have enough to meet your retirement goals? If you want to travel around the world but need more money to get to Australia, you might want to keep working for a little longer.
- **How is your health?** Unfortunately, you can't fight aging. There may come a time when you don't have the energy to continue working or it becomes too difficult physically to do so. If that's the case, you might need to slow down or stop working completely.
- **Do you have a new partner?** Maybe, after years of singlehood, you've found a partner who wants to settle down — with you and with retirement. Perhaps your plans didn't include someone new, but now this new person is making a life of leisure seem more appealing.
- **Are you newly single?** It sometimes takes a major life event to make a major life change. If you're recently divorced or bereaved, you might decide that life is too short and you don't want to keep working. You'll need to be sure that you have enough cash before retiring, but a large divorce settlement or life insurance policy could be enough to get you to punch your last time card.

Saving today for a Great Tomorrow

We've already talked a lot about how important it is to save, and we've given you some ideas on how to go about getting started. But we can't emphasize enough how critical it is to start investing early. Just look at the numbers: If you put $50,000 into an account that earns a 5 percent annual return, you'll have $216,097 after 30 years. Invest that same amount with only 10 years until retirement, and you'll have $81,444. Now consider what would happen if you saved an initial $50,000, but then contributed $10,000 every year for the next 30 years with the same 5 percent annualized return. You'll end up with a solid $913,705.

While stocks have, over time, always gone up, you can't simply rely on achieving big returns to fund your retirement. Sure, your portfolio could rise by 20 percent one year, but it could fall by 10 percent the next. The only surefire way to grow your savings is to put more in every year. The combination of long-term positive returns and continued investment is the best way to achieve your goals.

RRSPs versus TFSAs

You don't need to be Warren Buffett to save for retirement, but it's a good idea to at least familiarize yourself with the two main types of retirement investment accounts: RRSP (registered retirement savings plan) and TFSA (tax-free savings account). We cover the important points in this section, but to find out a lot more, read *Personal Finance For Canadians* (Wiley).

Tax-free versus tax-deferred

The one main reason why people have an RRSP or a TFSA or both is that they don't have to pay annual tax on what's inside these registered accounts. Money saved in a non-registered account is subject to a variety of taxes, including on any investment gains and dividend income.

An RRSP is a *tax-deferred account* because you pay tax on any money taken out of the account. How much you pay depends on your marginal tax rate. If you're in the highest tax bracket, you could get dinged for 50 percent of the withdrawal. A TFSA, on the other hand, is a true *tax-free account*, which means you won't pay a cent to the taxman on any withdrawals.

Why is one account tax-deferred and the other tax-free? You're saving pre-tax income in an RRSP and after-tax income in a TFSA. That's also why you get a tax refund when investing in an RRSP: What you put in reduces your taxable income dollar for dollar. If you owe taxes, like self-employed individuals would, an RRSP contribution could put you in a lower tax bracket. If you've already forked over your taxes, like most people do in every paycheque, you'll get some of the money back you've already paid. So, you haven't paid tax on the money inside the RRSP, which means you need to pay tax on it later, when you remove it from the account. The TFSA is tax-free because that dough has already been taxed.

Withdrawal methods

The other main difference between these two accounts is the way you can withdraw from them. You can pull money out of a TFSA at any time and recontribute those funds later. (However, to avoid getting penalized, you must wait until January 1 of the following year after you removed your funds to put them back in.) Because you can remove funds whenever you want and without having to pay tax, the TFSA is more versatile than the RRSP. You can use it for shorter-term goals, such as that new car you want to buy in five years, or for longer-term retirement goals.

Withdrawing from an RRSP is more complicated because the government set it up explicitly for retirement savings. They don't want you to move money out of it if you don't absolutely have to. With that in mind, any money withdrawn is subject to tax.

Because the government wants you to pay that tax, it withholds 10 percent of any withdrawals up to $5,000, 20 percent of any withdrawals between $5,000 and $15,000, and 30 percent of withdrawals over $15,000. (Note: These amounts vary slightly in Quebec. A withdrawal up to $5,000 is 21 percent, between $5,001 and $15,000 is 26 percent, and above $15,001 is 31 percent.) You could get some of that back if you end up in a lower tax bracket. However, you could also end up owing more, depending on how much income you earn that year.

In addition, you permanently lose the *contribution room,* the amount of money you're allowed to save in your RRSP every year. So, if you take out $50,000, you'll never get that $50,000 back. (Your room will still increase year after year, but your total room will forever be down by the amount of the withdrawal.)

When you turn 71, you must convert your RRSP into a RRIF (registered retirement income fund), at which point you need to withdraw a certain percent of those funds every year. These withdrawals must begin in the calendar year that you turn 72. You can employ a lot of different tax-planning strategies when you withdraw — including putting any funds you don't need into a TFSA — so talk to an advisor to understand the best options for your financial situation.

Deciding which account is right for you

Which account is best for you? That's one of the main financial planning questions, and one that has no definitive answer. If you can, you should max out both.

A key consideration when it comes to an RRSP is how much you're making now and how much you'll be earning in retirement. The point of an RRSP is to invest in the years you're in a high tax bracket and withdraw when you're in a lower one. Why? Because you'll pay less tax in those high earning years thanks to the RRSP's tax-deduction power, and you'll owe less on the withdrawals because you'll be in a lower tax bracket.

Historically, this strategy has been easy to employ because most people need less income in retirement, so their tax bill should be lower than in their working years. However, now that more people are earning money into their 70s, many are paying a much larger tax bill on their withdrawals.

If you think you're going to earn a lot more later in life, you might start with a TFSA. But as you'll see in the following handy chart, you can save a lot more in an RRSP:

	RRSP	TFSA
Yearly contribution limit	18% of income earned in the previous year up to a maximum of $29,210 in 2022	$6000
Taxable	Pre-tax dollars are invested; growth and capital are taxed upon withdrawal	After-tax dollars are invested; growth is never taxed
Contribution carried forward	Until you turn 71	Forever
Minimum age	Whenever you start earning an income and paying taxes	18
Contribution	Pre-tax dollars	After-tax dollars
Tax refund	Yes	No
Withdrawal penalties	Yes, must pay withholding taxes and lose contribution room	No, as long as you don't recontribute during the same year you withdraw
Maximum lifetime contribution	Depends on your age and income	$81,500 in 2022

TIP

Here's a little chart to help you decide which account is right for you. Of course, the choice may be more nuanced than this, so talk to a professional before investing:

I will need the money soon	TFSA
I don't need money until retirement	RRSP
I earn a high income today	RRSP
I earn less than $30,000 a year	TFSA
I have more than $6,000 to save per year	RRSP

Drawing down savings

Married people have certain tax-planning strategies that they can deploy when it's time to withdraw their savings. For instance, retirees can give their spouse or common-law partner up to 50 percent of their eligible pension income so one person doesn't have to pay an exorbitant amount of tax. Couples can also use a spousal RRSP, which offers tax advantages to married and common-law partners.

Because of the lack of income-splitting and tax-reducing options available to single people, it's important to carefully plan retirement-related withdrawals so that you don't get hit with a hefty tax bill. You should work with an advisor or an accountant to develop a proper withdrawal strategy. Meanwhile, here are a few quick things to consider:

- If you end up withdrawing more money from a RRIF than you need to live on, put the excess into a TFSA, where it can continue to grow tax-free.
- Remove only the minimum required amount from your RRIF, unless you need more to live on.
- Minimize how much other income you earn so you don't get pushed into a higher tax bracket when you withdraw.

Younger people can also withdraw money from their RRSP to save for a home. The Homer Buyer's Plan lets you remove up to $35,000 from your RRSP tax-free as long as the money is going towards buying your first home. You have to pay back that money over the next 15 years. If you don't pay it back, you'll have to pay tax on the withdrawal.

In January 2023, you can also start saving in a new tax-free first home savings account (FHSA). You can save $8,000 a year, up to $40,000 total. Unused contribution room doesn't carry forward. Like an RRSP, contributions are tax deductible on the way in, but like a TFSA, you don't have to pay tax on those funds when you withdraw. Here are some other things to know about the FHSA:

- You must use the funds within 15 years of opening the account.
- If you don't use the funds within the allotted time, they can go into your RRSP, even if you don't have contribution room. Funds can also be transferred from your RRSP into your FHSA.
- To use the FHSA, you must be a resident of Canada and be at least 18 years of age. You are not allowed to have owned a home anytime in the year that the account nor during the preceding four calendar years.
- Any withdrawals not used to purchase a first home count as taxable income.

4

Budgeting for Your Best Life

Everyone hates budgeting, or at least they think they do — it's no fun watching your nickels and dimes or worrying about spending too much on a night out. Budgeting, though, gets a bad rap. Yes, reviewing bills and adding up expenses wouldn't appear next to the word *fun* in a dictionary, but creating a good budget and then sticking to it can be liberating. Do it right and not only will you never have to worry about running out of money but it'll be much easier to save for retirement, take a big trip, and go out to eat guilt-free.

But you can do all that without a budget, you say? Maybe so, but if you don't know where your money is going, one big purchase or unexpected event could send you into a debt spiral.

A lot of people think budgeting is for people who need to live frugally, but that's not true. In fact, creating a budget might allow you to spend more money on the things you care about the most. In this chapter, you examine how to create a budget, the costs of various expenses, why some things are pricier for single people, and how best to stick to your plan.

Recording Your Income

Budgeting begins with income. You need to know how much you have before you can figure out where to put it. If you listened to us in Chapter 3 and created a cash flow statement, you already know how much you're bringing in each month. If you skipped to this chapter or need a quick reminder on how to calculate income, add up all the money you earn in a month. That includes your monthly after-tax salary, stock dividend payments that go into your bank account, rental income, dollars you make from your side hustle — any liquid cash that you can potentially spend.

Put the number in a spreadsheet, such as Excel or Google Sheets, or use one of several budgeting apps and websites that allow you to record income and expenses and set spending limits in different categories. We recommend the budget planner from the Government of Canada at `https://itools-ioutils.fcac-acfc.gc.ca/BP-PB/budget-planner`.

Calculating Your Expenses

One of the main reasons you create a budget is to see how much you're spending in different areas of your life. You can then see if you're spending too much overall, in which case you can cut back on your expenses more generally or adjust your spending levels in different categories. For instance, maybe you'd rather cancel a few digital subscriptions services and allocate those funds to more nights out.

Organizing your expenses, which we talk much more about in Chapter 3, is not as hard as it looks. The easiest way is to go through your credit and debit card statements and see how much you spend on different things in a typical month. You don't need to go through an entire year's worth of statements, but also don't choose December, which will likely have higher expense than normal (presents, parties, travel, and so on). Jot down each expense under its appropriate heading, such as utilities, mortgage, internet, groceries, property taxes, car loans, and entertainment. When you're finished, you'll have a good idea of where your money is going each month.

Accounting for Goals

Knowing how you're spending your money now is only one part of budgeting. You also need to know how you're going to spend your cash in the future. If you just read Chapter 3, you'll have already thought about your short-term and long-term goals, and you might have attached numbers to how much it will cost to reach them. If not, think about what you want to spend your money on today (a new car, a big trip, a 75-inch TV) and what kind of retirement you might want in the future.

Calculate how much each goal will cost. Then decide when you want to reach each goal, and calculate how much you'll need to save per month to get there. Add that amount to your spreadsheet.

Budgeting Begins

Now that you know your income, expenses, and goals, you can create a budget. Here's how to start.

Step 1: Add your expenses and income. You've already done this this step if you created a cash flow statement (see Chapter 3). If not, calculate your total income and expenses to see if you're covering all your costs.

Step 2: Review your categories. Now look at how much you're spending in each category. Does what you're spending make sense? Perhaps you didn't realize just how much those visits to Winners were costing you.

Step 3: Create a category for savings. Most budgeters forget to account for savings. It's not really an expense, but it is money you need to deduct from your paycheque every month. Allocate some of your income to this category.

Step 4: Examine your goals. In the context of all your other savings and spending, see how much it will cost to achieve your many goals.

Step 5: Start moving things around. After you've completed the previous steps, the fun begins. It's time prioritize your spending. Mortgage or rent usually tops the list because you need a place to live. Note that you won't have much wiggle room with your day-to-day expenses (mortgage or rent, utilities, and groceries) because the costs likely stay the same each month. Next, look at your discretionary categories — eating out, travel, movies — and start cutting back if necessary. Also consider the designation of funds for each of your goals.

Most likely, you'll need to make some adjustments to the way you spend today. And that's okay — if you really want to travel next December, you'll probably be fine going out one less night a week. If you never use cable, you might want to cancel it and put the funds into your long-term investment account. Life is about balance (we're not going to say sacrifice), and budgeting helps you find that financial balance.

Two other categories to consider are an emergency savings fund and an opportunity fund. An *emergency fund* is critical; it's an account that you can tap into if an unexpected expense or situation pops up, such as a layoff, a medical issue, or a house repair. It's recommended that you save an amount equal to three to six months of your salary in an emergency fund in case you're without income for a while. If you don't allocate money to an emergency fund, you could end up blowing through your budget and racking up debt, making it hard to get back on track.

An *opportunity fund* is for those who may want to splurge on something down the road but aren't sure what they want to purchase yet. You might want to use the money in your opportunity fund to invest in a friend's business, purchase a rental property, or buy an expensive set of golf clubs. Add to this category after you've covered the rest of your expenses and goals.

Now that we've covered the basics of budgeting, let's get into more specific spending categories.

Groceries: The Stuff of Life

Everyone needs to eat. But how much do you need to spend on eating every month? According to the 2021 Canada's Food

Price Report, the average man between 31 and 50 spends about $296 dollars on groceries per month, while the average woman spends about $266. That amount is in line with the per person cost for an average family of four, which spends about $1,158 a month, or $289 a person. Of course, those numbers can vary widely depending on where you shop and what you eat.

The newly single might need to adjust some of their grocery spending. Unless you have children, you might not need to buy in bulk at Costco anymore, and you can probably forgo the large-sized lean ground beef you used to use for tacos. Do you need four litres of milk now or could one suffice?

Keeping costs down when prices soar

As we're writing this book, the annual inflation rate is at its highest point in more than three decades, so prices on everything from gas to lumber to food are rising rapidly. In February 2022, food prices climbed 7.2 percent year-over-year, with the price of meat, beef, and chicken rising even higher. Inflation is making it hard for many people to cover their food costs. Fortunately, you can do a few things to lower your grocery bills:

- **Shop at a cheaper grocery store.** Although every grocery store carries the same food essentials, prices vary by chain. According to MoneyGenius.ca (`www.moneygenius.ca`), a pound of ground beef costs

$2.29 more at Loblaws than at No Frills. Generally, No Frills, FreshCo, and Food Basics are the least expensive, while Safeway, Sobeys, and Loblaws are the most expensive. Not every item is cheaper at No Frills than Loblaws, so make sure what you're buying is indeed less expensive at another grocery before switching. (Store names don't sound familiar? Some have different monikers in the west than the east, so do a quick internet search to find the brand name in your area.)

- **Cut back on sizes.** As mentioned, you might not need the large-sized package of meat or the biggest milk carton. If you find yourself freezing a lot of food, consider buying a bit less now so your monthly cash flow remains manageable.
- **Consider coupons.** Grocery stores issue coupons for all kinds of items. Many coupons are online instead of in a physical flyer, so check your store's website to see the deals.
- **Check into meal planning.** Using an app to plan meals is another good way to keep costs under control. Many meal-planning apps are preloaded with recipes and grocery lists, making it easier to purchase only what you need and ensuring that nothing is wasted, including your hard-earned dollars.

TIP: Check out these popular meal-planning apps: Paprika (www.paprikaapp.com), Mealime (www.mealime.com), and MealPrepPro (www.mealpreppro.com).

Splurging on occasion

There will likely come a time when you want to splurge on a high-priced item, such as an assortment of expensive cheeses. Our advice? Go for it: Everyone needs to live a little. But consider your budget before you buy. If you want to exceed your grocery costs by $200, think about pairing back elsewhere for that month so your income and expenses continue to align. If you're hankering to throw a party, consider dipping into your opportunity fund, which is designed for this type of previously unplanned moment.

Trimming Utility Costs

Utility costs vary by province and home type — older homes with poor insulation result in more expensive bills than new builds, for instance — but here's what the average Ontarian pays per month, according to MovingWaldo.com (www.movingwaldo.com):

Gas	$46
Water	$64
Electricity	$95

Utilities are one expense that's easier to cover as a couple. If you were spending $500 a month heating your home before a divorce, you're still going to spend $500 a month after it because the cost relates more to the size of the home than the people living there. That said, in this section we cover some ways to lower your bills.

Reducing energy consumption

You're going to pay more if you let the heat or AC run full blast all day and night. One simple cost-cutting measure is to lower the heat or turn off the AC when you're not home. At night, grab an extra blanket and decrease your home's temperature.

TIP

Consider installing a smart thermostat, which enables you to control your home's temperature remotely and set the temperature according to the time of day. For instance, you could program the thermostat to drop to 15 degrees during the day, rise to 19 degrees before you get home from work, and fall to 14 degrees when you're tucked in bed at night. According to Nest, the most popular smart thermostat brand, these devices can save up to 12 percent on heating costs and 15 percent on cooling fees. Its users report an average annual savings of between $131 and $145. Ecobee, a Canadian brand, says its users save up to 26 percent on utility costs.

Reining in your water usage

Unlike utility costs, water costs should come down a bit when you're on your own because you're charged for usage. You should report your water reading once a year because you could get money back for water you paid for but didn't use. The municipal bodies that oversee water usage usually estimate how much you're using. If the meter reading indicates you used less, you'll get a credit on your account. However, it could show that you used more, which may trigger an additional payment.

In any case, shut off the taps when you brush your teeth, don't run your sprinklers for too long in the summer, and if you notice that your bill is unusually high, call a plumber to see if you have a leak somewhere.

Managing your electricity

Take a similar approach with electricity as you do with water and heating. Turn off the lights when you leave a room or the house, and consider buying smart light bulbs, switches, and outlets that you can turn off from an app. Wait until you have a full load of laundry before you turn on the washer or dryer, and turn off any electronics, such as your TV, if they're not being used.

Life on the Go: Transportation

Planes, Trains, and Automobiles isn't just one of the more hilarious John Candy movies ever made, it's also the way you get around. Add walking, biking, busing, and electric scootering to the mix, too. While being single doesn't necessarily affect your methods of transportation, some people may need to buy a car after a divorce or find ways to cut down on transportation costs. In this section, we outline some different transportation options and their effect on your finances, so that you can ensure that you're getting from point A to point B efficiently and cost effectively.

Deciding whether to lease or buy

Do you want a new car every four years or are you content to have the same ride for the next decade? That's often how people decide on whether to lease or buy their car. What you choose, though, could have a significant effect on your budget and cash flow.

It's a lot more fun to lease a car because you'll get a new one every few years. You also don't have to worry about fixing it when the warranty runs out because maintenance costs are generally covered throughout the lease. Another plus: The monthly payments are usually cheaper with leasing than buying because you're paying to use the car for a predetermined amount of time, typically two to four years.

The main downside of leasing is that you never own the asset outright. Besides the monthly payments, there may be other costs associated with leasing, such as kilometre (km) restrictions — go over the limit and you could end up paying per extra km used. If want to return the car before your lease is up, you might have to pay an early lease termination fee and wear and tear charges.

Leasing a car is a lot like renting property, while owning a car is similar to buying a home. With the former you're always making payments; with the latter, you're paying down a loan to zero. Unfortunately, cars aren't like houses in one crucial way: They don't appreciate in value, so you'll end up paying more for your vehicle than you'll get back for it when you eventually sell. Still, once you pay off the loan, you can allocate that monthly payment to other parts of your budget.

Your monthly car loan payment depends on four factors: the price of the car, the interest rate on the loan, the term of the loan, and the down payment you make on the car.

Unfortunately, you can't really shop around for the best rate because you'll typically finance your car through the dealership. (Another option is to use a personal line of credit from your bank.) Car loan rates can depend on your credit rating — the lower your rating, the higher the rate — but dealerships often offer low-interest and even zero-interest loans to entice you to buy your car from them.

Maintenance is the other factor to keep in mind when buying, although you'll likely get a three-to-five-year worry-free warranty, and you can buy an extended warranty.

So, what's the best option? If you're going to hang on to your car after your payments end, you'll come out ahead with buying. If you care only about the monthly cash flow, you might want to lease. But if you have the cash, the best option is to buy a new car outright so that you don't pay interest or have ongoing monthly payments.

Comparing insurance costs

The next step after buying a car is getting insurance. Canada's car insurance regime varies by provide. British Columbia, Saskatchewan, Manitoba, and Quebec have public insurance, while the other provinces have private options. Public insurance is run by the government, so pricing is straightforward. With private insurance, different companies compete on price and service, which means you can shop around to find the best deal.

In either case, payments are typically based on your driving record (you'll have a higher bill if you've racked up a few speeding tickets), your age (younger drivers are riskier), the kind of car you drive (sports cars are riskier in the insurance company's eyes), and whether you're driving your car to work or keeping it at home (the former costs more). Rates also vary by province: B.C. has the highest average insurance premium at $1,832, according to the Insurance Bureau of Canada, while Quebec is the cheapest at $717 per year.

Taking advantage of ride sharing

Most Canadians have taken an Uber or a Lyft at some point, likely when going home after a late night out at the bar. Some people, though, are forgoing car ownership in favour of using ride-sharing services to do everything from getting groceries to going to work. Whether you can save money relying on an Uber or using a rent-by-the-hour vehicle such as Zipcar is up for debate, though reports say ridesharing could be cost effective if you drive less than 16,000 km a year.

The way to go: public transportation

Depending on where you live, buses, subways, trains, and streetcars may be the best option of them all. A monthly bus pass in Winnipeg, for instance, costs $106, while a year-long subway pass in Toronto will run you $146 per month. Public transportation is a great option for single people who live in an urban area close to transit. In Ontario, those living outside Toronto can also take the Go Train, while those near Vancouver can take the SkyTrain.

Going green: Cycling or walking

Walking is good for the mind, body, and wallet. Other than the price of a good pair of shoes, it costs nothing to get your legs moving. Of course, unless you live close to everything you need, walking won't solve all your transit needs, but the more you can move, the more you can save.

Cycling has become a go-to transportation method for a lot of urban dwellers, especially since the advent of e-bikes, which are equipped with a motor that propels riders. The average e-bike costs about $4,750, but that's still cheaper than the total cost of a car.

One problem with walking and biking in Canada is the weather. Make sure to get warm winter clothing if these are your primary modes of transportation.

Funding Your Digital Life

Today, a lot of our cash flow goes towards all kinds of digital experiences, including phones, digital watches, streaming services, online storage space, and Candy Crush gold bars. While we now need a lot of these services in our daily lives, it's also easy to subscribe to something, forget about it, and then continue paying monthly for that unused app.

TIP Review your subscriptions on a regular basis and cancel the ones you don't use. Consider tossing those dollars into your opportunity fund.

Exploring cell phone options

A cell phone can be more expensive if you're a single person because a lot of carriers have plans where you can share minutes and data with family members, making the overall per person cost of a mobile less expensive. Canada, which has one of the highest wireless costs in the world, has only three main carriers: Rogers, Bell, and Telus.

Although your choices are limited, shop around to find a plan that works best for your situation. You might not need to pay for North-American-wide calling if you primarily use WhatsApp to communicate with your long-distance friends. You'll probably need some data, but if you don't plan on watching Netflix on your phone, you might not need the gold star plan.

In addition, pay-as-you-go options and some so-called discount carriers, such as Fido and Koodo (owned by Rogers and Telus, respectively, so they're not really discount carriers per se) are sometimes less expensive.

If you want a better deal from your current carrier, ask for the retention department and see what they'll do to keep you as a customer.

Life is nothing without the internet

The internet should really go under the "utilities" category because it's now as important as heating and water to people's lives. Like with cell phones, Canada boasts some of the most expensive internet rates on the planet because there's barely any competition. Rogers, Bell, Telus, and Shaw (which is in the midst of an acquisition by Rogers) are the main players, though several smaller ones cater to rural areas.

Reducing an internet bill will take some effort, including spending too long on the phone waiting for customer service, but it's worth calling once a year to see if your company is offering any discounts. Some bundle TV, mobile, and internet, which can bring down the cost of each individual service. Shop around to see if there are any new-customer offers. If nothing else works, tell your provider you want to cancel; they'll often give you a discount to entice you to stick around.

Subscribing to online entertainment

Surveys find that we spend around $200 per month on online services, making digital subscriptions one of our biggest monthly expenses. These costs are also starting to rise;

a standard Netflix subscription, for instance, now costs $16.49 per month, up from $9.99 a month in 2016. If you subscribe to many streaming services, a music service, such as Spotify or Apple Music, and a file storage service, such as Dropbox or iCloud, the costs can really start to add up.

When you're creating your budget, think carefully about whether you need all these services. How badly must you watch that one show on Disney+? Is it worth $11.99 per month? Also review the rest of your subscriptions to see what you might not be using. Does it still make sense to pay for the Google Drive storage space you bought three years ago? You can save hundreds of dollars a year just by reigning in your digital expenses.

The Freedom of Independent Travel

Feel like going on a trip to Hawaii? Well, if you're single, you can — at least without having to check with anyone else's schedule. It can be a lot of fun to go away where and when you want to, but you'll have to pay extra to go it alone.

No matter your status, you'll pay the same price for your flight, but hotels are generally more expensive for single people than couples. We looked at Expedia.ca for hotels in Hawaii between December 24 and December 31, 2022, which is peak travel time. During that week, a night at the Outrigger Reef Waikiki Beach Resort costs $459 for one room with two people. The cost of that same room for one person? $459 a night. A few other searches did show some discounts for one person versus two, but the difference was $50 a night at most.

The situation is the same with a rental car. The price is generally the same whether it's one person or two, although sometimes a second driver costs a little more.

Some resorts cater to singles, but they're not any less expensive because you're paying for an experience. The resorts are also hoping that you'll spend more on drinks and food as you mingle with other guests.

If you want to cut back on travel expenses, consider an Airbnb. You can often rent entire homes for the cost of a standard hotel room. Or if you're on a tighter budget, look into renting a room in a house. Other ways to travel include camping, glamping, and motelling. (You'll have plenty of newly renovated chic motels to choose from.)

Whatever you spend your money on, whether it's jet setting, a new mobile phone, a steak splurge, or something else, just make sure it fits within your budget.

5

Deciding Where to Lay Your Head

Whether you own or rent, live in a large country home or a compact urban condo, housing will likely make up the biggest expense in your household budget. If you own the home you live in outright, it's easily your biggest asset, and one you need to carefully manage for today and the future. As real estate prices linger at all-time highs, the cost and financial implications of where you live loom larger than ever.

If you're newly single, a change in your living arrangements may be in order. A lot of divorces end up with the now ex-spouses selling their abode, largely because it can be expensive to maintain a large home on one income (especially if you're the one paying spousal support). And there may be mounting debts and expensive lawyers' fees to pay off, too.

Losing a spouse could result in move, too. You might realize that you don't need as large a space, or maybe it's too hard to live in the same spot without your significant other.

It's important to think carefully about where you want to live because your home plays a prominent role not only in your financial picture but also in your everyday life.

Deciding Where You Want to Live

If you're making a change in your living situation, it's easy to get caught up in the aesthetics of a wraparound porch, a grand staircase, or smart amenities. Bidding wars, meanwhile, have a way of making people overspend on a house, condo, or cottage. Deciding on where to live, however, shouldn't start with the home décor or be made under pressure.

Instead, start with the big picture. Imagine the life you want to live and can reasonably afford. Are you a walker? If you move to a neighbourhood with no sidewalks and faraway stores, you may find yourself with restless legs. Are you unable or unwilling to do the upkeep on a home or pay others to do so? Don't be seduced with that 100-year-old Victorian.

Most importantly, if you overextend to pay for a dream home, your ability to afford other lifestyle perks such as eating out, travel, and hobbies could be affected. Cash flow is king, so it's important to make sure that you align your budget with your retirement plans before you buy.

Moving, though, can be a lot of fun and provide the fresh start you might need. Just keep the costs and hassle of finding a new place in mind.

It's often said that it's best to wait a year after a life change to make any big decisions, and dealing with your living arrangements can fall in this category. Look to friends, family, and financial professionals for advice, support, and endless drives around favourite neighbourhoods to suss out properties. Then make a decision that makes financial sense for you now and into the future.

The Pros and Cons of Buying

Canadians love their real estate, with nearly 68 percent of Canadians owning their own homes. That percentage may decline if housing prices remain stratospheric, but many Canadians make home ownership a top life goal when they're younger and then do all they can to make those mortgage payments.

The benefits of home ownership are numerous, and not all are financial. Here are a few:

- **Equity building:** As discussed in Chapter 2, owning a home contributes a significant amount to your net worth. As you pay down your mortgage and real estate values go up — as they have at a steady clip over the last several decades — you can build a significant amount of equity in your home. When it comes time to sell, you could make a lot of money, which you could then use to fund your retirement goals. While you never know what will happen in the future, a lot of boomers have funded big chunks of their retirement from the proceeds of a sale.

- **Sense of control:** A big reason why so many people love owning their own home is precisely because it's their own. You're in the driver's seat. You can decide to take down a wall, put in a new backsplash, and importantly, sell and move on when you choose. For a lot of newly single people, this is exactly the kind of fresh start they need.
- **Potential for rental income:** Being a landlord can be lucrative, especially if you have a desirable home in a good neighbourhood. A lot of people, especially those in major urban centres, are looking to rent basement apartments, a floor of a house, or even just a room. As we're writing this, a lot of basement rentals in Toronto, for instance, are renting for between $1,200 and $2,000 a month.
- **Tax credits:** Homeowners may also be eligible for some tax credits. For instance, the Home Buyers' Amount

(someone tell the CRA to come up with better credit monikers) lets you claim up to $5,000 of the purchase of a home, as long as you did not own a house in the year you bought the new place and in the four preceding years. You might also be eligible for a GST/HST rebate if you bought a new or substantially renovated home from a builder. It may also be possible to write off some expenses related to rental income. Tax laws are complicated, so be sure to check out `www.canada.ca/en/revenue-agency/services/tax/individuals/segments/homeowners.html` for more information.

Of course, home ownership has pitfalls as well. Here are a few of the cons to owning your own abode:

- **Lack of flexibility:** If you suddenly want to move, you'll have to be patient — snapping your fingers won't get you out of your house or condo. You'll have to do small repairs and then stage the place before you sell, and also hope the market doesn't slow down right when you list.
- **Responsibility:** It's your place, which mean you have to maintain it — and that can get expensive. Common repairs include replacing a hot water tank, fixing a roof, and buying a new furnace — and there's always some weird water leak that needs attention. Then there's snow removal, lawn care, cleaning the

eavestroughs, and more, which you have to do yourself of pay someone else to do. If you own a condo, you typically pay condo fees to cover building upkeep and maintenance.

- **Taxes and insurance:** There's more to home ownership than a mortgage and maintenance. You also need to pay property taxes and insure your home from theft and fire. The tax amount varies by city, but Vancouverites, who own the most expensive homes in the country, will be happy to know that they pay the least amount of property tax in the land.
- **Easy to overextend:** It's tempting in a buyers' market to overextend and get into a home you can barely afford. Doing that can make you house poor and leave you sitting on the couch while your pals hit the links and stamp their passports. If interest rates go up, your mortgage costs could rise. If you have a variable-rate mortgage, that bump will be almost immediate. If you have a fixed-rate mortgage, you'll have to pay more when it comes to time to renew your term, which is usually every five years. If something happens to your home or property that requires a significant investment to fix — and it's not covered by insurance — you could struggle to cover the costs.

The Pros and Cons of Renting

Us real-estate-loving Canadians sometimes overlook renting as a way to approach our housing needs. If you've been raised to believe that the only path to a happy and financially sound life is through home ownership, it can be tricky to ponder the upsides of renting.

But upsides there are. Especially for single people later in life, renting offers significant benefits:

- **Flexibility:** Renters can usually move on with just 30 days' notice. Tell the landlord and then pack up — that's it. It's ideal for single people who may now be free to lug their laptop to a new locale every few months, want to downsize when the kids leave home, or would like to eventually move to a place that offers additional support, such as a retirement home.
- **Fewer responsibilities:** The single best part of renting is that you don't have to put up any cash to fix a broken sink. Roof leaks? Call the landlord. Furnace stops working? Call the landlord. Light switch stops working? Call the . . . you get the idea. Property care, snow removal, and all those tasks are someone else's responsibility. That makes renting a strong choice for those who find such chores stressful or physically challenging.

- **Frees up capital:** If you've sold a home and have decided to rent, you'll now have access to your nest egg. Although you still have to pay the landlord every month — and renting can be as much or more expensive than owning depending on where you live and the interest rate — you'll still have money from the sale of your home to fund your lifestyle.

Everything, of course, has its pros and cons, and there are a few downsides to renting:

- **Lack of equity:** It's hard to build your net worth when renting. Home ownership essentially forces you to save by paying down a mortgage. That, combined with rising property values, makes it fairly easy to build up equity in your abode. With renting, you're helping someone else grow their net worth.
- **Increasing payments:** While home owners can potentially have fluctuating mortgage payments — with a variable-rate mortgage or when it comes time to renew a fixed rate — renters' payments can rise every year. Typically, landlords can legally increase rents by between 1 percent and 2 percent per year depending on the province, so expect your payments to go up.
- **Lack of control**: Landlords sometimes put profits before people and may be lax with upkeep or repairs. You also risk being evicted through no fault of your own, so the

landlord's family member can move in or because they want to fix up the place and charge more (the illustrious renoviction). Many jurisdictions in Canada do not have strong laws protecting renters, and many tenants can find themselves in conflicts with their landlords that are difficult to resolve.

Making the Most Out of Your Mortgage

Given that this is a personal finance book, we can't go any further without talking a bit about mortgages. As you see in Chapter 6, a mortgage is the kind of debt that you may want to have, in that the more you pay it down, the more your nest egg will grow. But you must also make sure that your monthly mortgage payments fit in your budget and, most importantly, your monthly cash flow.

An old rule of thumb says that no more than 30 percent of your income should go toward housing expenses, which includes mortgage principal, interest, property taxes, utilities costs, and condo fees (if you pay them). As housing prices have climbed, a lot of people are allocating a lot more than 30 percent of their income. A National Bank of Canada report found that in the fourth quarter of 2021, Canadians were spending 48.6 percent of their income, on average, to service their mortgage.

That number could continue to rise. As we write this in March 2022, Canadian real estate is still breaking records. The average home now costs about $816,000, up 20 percent from where it was a year earlier. Of course, that number could decline —many experts have bet on a Canadian real estate crash the last several years, but with the country's population rising and interest rates remaining relatively low, those experts have continually been proven wrong.

Understanding interest rates

If you're going to own a home, you need to know a little bit about interest rates. So sit up and pay attention, or at least try not to fall asleep for the next few paragraphs.

The Bank of Canada (BoC) is a crown corporation responsible for setting monetary policy in the country. BoC oversees the *overnight rate,* which is the rate that banks and other financial institutions must charge when borrowing money from one another. That rate ties into all kinds of other interest rates, including the rate at which companies can borrow, how much you'll owe on your line of credit debt, and what kind of rate you can get for a mortgage.

The rate can fluctuate depending on what's happening in the world. In recessions, such as in 2008 and 2020, the BoC slashed rates to the ultra-low level of 0.25 percent to encourage borrowing. The thinking is that if rates are super low, people and businesses will take on more debt (because the interest on that debt is almost nothing) and then put that cheap money back into the economy via equipment purchases (for businesses), televisions sets and more (for consumers), or mortgages (for both).

When the economy strengthens again, the BoC starts to raise rates to discourage overborrowing. Why would they do that? Because if people borrow and then spend too much, retailers will raise their prices (more demand and less supply equals increasing costs), creating inflation. The BoC, at least in theory, is always trying find an equilibrium between an economy that is too hot or too cold.

Housing prices have soared over the last decade for a lot of reasons (such as not enough supply and wealthy non-Canadian buyers looking for investment properties), but one of the main reasons is that interest rates have been so low for so long. Think about it: Since 2008, the overnight rate has not climbed above 1.75 percent. Prior to the Great Recession, the BoC's rate was above 4 percent! With borrowing costs so cheap for so long, it's no surprise that the average Canadian home price has risen significantly over the past 14 years.

Interest rates will play a big factor in your monthly mortgage payments and in the price you pay for a home. When rates are low, your money goes a little further because more of it is going to the principal rather than the interest. And this is exactly why housing prices have climbed: If you had to pay

5 percent interest on a $800,000 loan with a 25-year amortization period, you'd owe the bank $4,652 per month. If you had to pay only 2 percent interest, you'd owe $3,387 a month. If your rate was a measly 1.25 percent, which is what Bryan's rate was when we wrote this book, you'd owe $3,105 a month. See where we're going here? If paying a 1.25 percent rate is easy, you might be far more willing to pay a higher price for a home than you would if you had to pay 5 percent. Multiply this scenario across the country and you get rising home prices.

Fixed versus variable rate

If you're in the market for a new home, you'll want to consider both fixed-rate and variable-rate mortgage options. (Remember, the *rate* is the interest you'll pay on the amount you borrow from the bank to help you finance the purchase of your home.) What you choose will depend on your risk tolerance level and your monthly cash flow.

A variable rate:

- Usually starts at a lower rate than fixed
- Increases every time the BoC hikes its rate, which will either increase your monthly payment or increase the amount of interest that gets paid from your current payment
- Decreases every time the BoC lowers its rate, which then decreases your monthly payment or lowers the

amount of interest that gets paid out of your current payment
- Results in a penalty of three months of interest if you break your mortgage before your term is up

A fixed rate:

- Usually is higher than a variable rate
- Requires you to lock in that rate for your entire term, which is typically 5 years, but can be 3 or 10
- Doesn't decrease when rates fall but also doesn't increase when rates rise
- Might require you to pay a higher penalty than with a variable-rate mortgage to get out of a mortgage term early

What people choose generally comes to down to whether they're comfortable taking the risk of having to pay higher payments as rates rise or if they prefer the cash flow certainty that comes with a fixed rate. In any case, you have to sign on for a new rate— either variable or fixed, you don't have to choose the same thing forever— when it comes time to renew your term.

Qualifying for a mortgage

Unless you have a big pile of cash lying around that you can use for purchasing a home, you'll need to qualify for a mortgage. Generally, dual-income families have an easier time getting approved because they have more money at their collective disposal to spend on their monthly payments. That said, those who are single with strong finances shouldn't have trouble qualifying either.

When applying for a mortgage, look for the best interest rate you can find. The process is much easier with a mortgage broker, who can go to multiple lenders to get the best rate for you. You can also go directly to a bank or lender, but it could take some time to shop around. In addition, several online sites, such as ratehub.ca (`www.ratehub.ca/`), list rates from various lenders. But what's on those sites may not be what you end up getting because the rate you'll receive is determined by a number of factors, such as credit score and how well you or your mortgage broker negotiates.

After you decide which lender you want to work with, you'll need to provide several pieces of information, including your assets, income, debt, and proof of employment. (Find out all you'll need at `www.canada.ca/en/financial-consumer-agency/services/mortgages/preapproval-qualify-mortgage.html`.)

Perhaps the most important part of all of this, though, relates to how much money you can qualify for. It used to be that you just had to comfortably cover your monthly payment, which was based on the rate the lender offered you. A few years ago, to cool housing prices and ensure that people could continue paying their mortgages when rates rise, the government introduced a stress test. You now have to show that you can cover a monthly payment based on a 5.25 percent rate (that number can change, so double-check) or the interest rate you negotiate with your lender plus 2 percent, whichever is higher. You'll end up paying a lower rate than that, but you still need to qualify at the higher rate.

If all your documents check out and you're able to meet the stress test requirements, you'll be approved for a mortgage. If you don't meet the stress test, you may need to ask for less of a loan, in which case you may need to buy a lower-priced home.

Creating more cash flow

Owning a home has several other advantages. One is that if rates fall, you can break your mortgage and re-sign at a lower rate. If you can get a lower monthly payment, you'll have more money to save for retirement or to fund your daily expenses. Although there's usually a penalty for breaking a mortgage, it may be worth it depending on the new rate.

Homeowners can also leverage the equity in their home by taking out a home equity line of credit (HELOC), which is like a line of credit with the rate based on your mortgage rate. A HELOC gives you access to up to 80 percent of the value of your home, minus your mortgage. You pay the loan back just as you would a line of credit. If you end up selling your home, you'll have to pay the HELOC back, plus any mortgage loans still outstanding.

You can tap into your home equity in other ways, too:

- **Reverse mortgage:** A reverse mortgage lets you take money from the equity you've built up in your home, but you can borrow a smaller percentage of your home's value compared to a HELOC. However, you usually don't have to pay off that loan or any monthly interest. Instead, the interest, which is usually fixed (unlike a HELOC, which is variable) accumulates, and you usually don't have to pay a cent back until you sell the house. There are some arrangements where interest can, and must, be paid back at regular intervals. If not, be careful that you don't let the loan grow too much over time; otherwise, there won't be much left after you sell.
- **Downsizing:** If you need money or are ready to move out of your home, you can sell your home and buy another one, we hope at a lower price. However, the concept of downsizing doesn't always work these days. A lot of people dream of selling their suburban home for a downtown condo, but in cities like Toronto and Vancouver, that city centre abode could be as expensive or even pricier than the place you sold. If you do have money left over after buying a new place, consider investing it in an RRSP (if you're younger than 71) or a TFSA, where it can grow on a tax-deferred or tax-free basis, respectively.

Making Other Housing Arrangements

Two great fallacies of life are that you either have to rent or own and that you must live with your immediate family in a house, a condo, or an apartment. Instead, you have myriad ways to put together a great but less conventional living arrangement. Here are some ideas:

- **Co-live.** You can buy into a home with others in what's called a co-living arrangement. In this situation, you have your own living quarters but shared communal indoor and outdoor spaces. Think communal garden, dining room, and guest room. These newer approaches to living can often be more affordable and come with a built-in community. However, be aware that some municipalities don't allow co-living, though advocates are trying to change these rules.
- **Rent in a co-op.** In a co-op, the tenants are the owners. That means no one will evict you for no reason, the rents will go up only if absolutely necessary, and you have a vote in how the co-op is run. These are great communities that often run social events and garden clean-up days. Few new co-ops have been

built in Canada in recent years and most have lengthy wait lists.

- **Live in a multigenerational setup.** If you're going to live with others, it might as well be those related to you. For many families, sharing a home or adjacent units is natural, especially if a parent becomes single. In that case, the parent might move in with an adult child and their family, or that younger brood will move to the family home.
- **Expand your space.** Many municipalities permit laneway houses and garden suites. If you have the space, investing in such a structure could allow you to become a homeowner and landlord at the same time. You can use the new space to house family members or even yourself. Doing this kind of expansion requires capital but offers an excellent investment over time. It also allows you to stay on your property and eventually lower your living costs.
- **Go off land.** People live in houseboats and floating shipping containers. They dwell in their recreational vehicles. Who says you need a piece of land at all?

If you're interested in a different type of living arrangement, note that there may be barriers to making it work:

- **Finances:** If you need a loan, banks may balk at your unique housing choice. If you can pay in cash, great.

But if you lack a mortgage or don't technically own where you live, it can be difficult to get a loan without collateral.

- **Rules:** Bylaws and other regulations could make your living arrangements mired in red tape or outright illegal. Before you move forward, find out what you can about the local rules, which can be found on city and provincial sites.
- **Reality:** Be sure to give yourself a reality check before doing anything too different. Do you really like living so closely to family or strangers? Will you miss out on any key hobbies or lifestyle choices due to where you live? There could be risk involved, either financially or via regulations, so be sure you're ready for what's ahead.

Relocating to a Popular Destination

If you can live anywhere in the world you want, why don't you? Canada is great, but the winters are chilly. The warmth and interesting cultures of other places entice many people, especially those in their post-working years. If you have family living outside Canada, you may want to finally spend more time with them, devoting a few months of the year with relatives. You won't be the only one coming and going: Every year, about a million Canadians head to the U.S. for the winter.

Thanks to laptops and Wi-Fi, you could become a digital nomad and work anywhere, basking in a new career or a semi-retirement that includes a few hours of work every day and then a golf game and a swim.

The following are some popular destinations to retire to outside Canada:

- **Belize:** English speaking and affordable; qualified retirement person program with a path to residency
- **Mexico:** Close to Canada; affordable healthcare; great food and climate; many regions speak English
- **Costa Rica:** Excellent healthcare; lots to do; affordable
- **Panama:** Great healthcare, safe streets, pension program for expats that comes with perks, such as discounts on movies, hotels, water service, and doctors
- **Portugal:** Residency programs provide EU access; great food and beaches

Living away for at least part of the year comes with certain financial and other complexities. It would be nice to come and go as you please, but it's not as easy as that. Here are a few things to consider:

- **Health coverage:** To remain enrolled in your provincial health insurance program, you must live at home for a set amount of time a year. If you're away too long, your coverage will lapse, and there will be a waiting period to get it back, if and when you return to Canada. As well, any privately purchased supplementary health insurance may become invalid. Ontario requires you to be physically in the province for 153 days over a 12-month period. In British Columbia, you need to be in the province for 5 or 6 months out of the year, depending on your situation.

- **Social security:** Getting your Canada Pension Plan (CPP) and Old Age Security (OAS) benefits could become more complicated if you move from Canada on a more permanent basis. To keep getting benefits, you need to be residing in a country with a social security agreement with Canada. Fortunately, Canada has agreements with dozens of countries, including Antigua and Barbuda, Australia, Barbados, Chile, France, India, South Korea, the United Kingdom, and the United States.
- **Taxes:** If you stay a long time in another country, you could be considered a resident for tax purposes. That determination depends on several factors, such as whether you maintain significant ties to Canada by owning property here, if you earn money in your new home, and how long you spend in the other country. If Canada has a tax treaty with the other country — as it

does with the U.S. — and you don't meet the substantial presence test for Canadian residency, you might be considered a resident for tax purposes and have to file and pay taxes.

TIP: Unlike healthcare, you don't just have to be in Canada for 183 days a year; what matters is how long you're in Canada over a three-year period. You need to get this calculation right, or you could owe taxes. Seek advice from a tax expert familiar with Canada and the country where you want to spend time.

If you rent a home in another country, that's one thing. Owning is quite another:

- **Ownership rules:** Some countries do not let noncitizens buy property. Know the local rules before you shop for real estate.
- **Taxes:** If you rent or sell your overseas property, you'll likely have to pay local taxes on the rental income or sale of the home, respectively.
- **Mortgage:** If you can't pay cash for your property, you may need to shop around for a Canadian lender that will help you out. Many banks with operations in the

U.S. will lend to Canadians buying there. Getting a mortgage could be more complex if you're buying in a different country.

- **Insurance:** Your insurance needs for your overseas property might be quite different than they are in Canada. There may be local rules regarding what type of coverage you must have, plus there could be specific risks related to the geography of your location — waterfront properties in particular have additional coverage needs. If you plan to rent your property when you're not there, you'll need liability insurance, too. If your property is going to sit vacant for weeks or months at a time, you'll likely need someone to check it regularly or risk losing coverage.
- **Estate planning:** We're sorry to go there, but if you die, your estate can get complex for your heirs. Many put ownership of foreign property into a trust to ensure a smoother transition.

If you're planning to become a snowbird, a digital nomad, or something in-between, protect yourself from financial and other challenges by working with an experienced team of professionals. Do your research, listen to their guidance, and make your travel and housing plans accordingly.

6

Managing Your Finances after a Divorce or Death

As the saying goes, life happens when you're busy making other plans. Most people don't get married thinking that they'll someday get divorced, and no one likes to think about losing a loved one. But when these things happen, they can affect your financial plans. For instance, your retirement may have been based on two incomes, but now you must reach your goals on one. Or you might have to consider selling your home and moving to a smaller one.

But a divorce or a death doesn't necessarily mean your plans will go off track. A life insurance policy might help you pay off your mortgage and allow you to keep the house, or spousal support payments could help you maintain your current lifestyle. In this chapter, we look at divorce and death, and the effect both can have on your finances.

Resetting Your Finances After a Divorce

Divorce tends to have a greater effect than death does on your finances. You may have to find and pay for a new place to live, as well as manage on one income instead of two. You might also have legal bills and child and spousal support payments. Meanwhile, the retirement goals you and your spouse were jointly saving towards might need to change. Whatever your situation, your finances will likely need a reset after a divorce.

Mine, yours, yours, mine: Dividing assets

Nothing says reset like having to divide assets down the middle. You might have bought most of the stuff in your house, or perhaps you were the one doing all the investing. Depending on when you were married and whether you had a prenuptial agreement, a marriage agreement, or both, you will likely have to hand over half your assets to your now ex-partner.

Generally, assets get split 50-50, but it's not quite as cut and dry as that. If your investment account has $500,000, and your spouse's account has $100,000, you don't have to hand over $250,000. Rather, you'd give them enough to bring their share in line with yours — so in this case you'd pay them $200,000 so that each of you have $300,000 in assets. When it comes to real estate, the easiest way to divide a home is to sell it and split the proceeds down the middle. But the other person could also buy you out of your share of the home, or vice versa, either with cash or by giving you other assets, such as a larger share of an RRSP. You'll also need to value other belongings you've accumulated over the years, such as furniture, jewellery, and electronics, and then split them evenly based on the dollar amount.

Debts also get divided. If you have $10,000 on your credit card, you must now pay $5,000 and your former partner will also have to pay $5,000. However, the credit card company isn't going to split the bill; they want to get paid by the person whose name is on the card. If you can't pay off the debt, you'll have to take out a line of credit and use it to pay your spouse that $5,000. You'll then have to pay off the $5,000 on the line of credit.

Remember, the name on the credit card is the person responsible for paying it off, so if your ex takes your $5,000 and spends it on a trip instead, it's still up to your ex to pay off the loan; you did your part by paying your half of the balance.

Only assets and debts accumulated from the date of the marriage or common-law relationship and the date you and your ex separated are divided. If you got married in your 20s, it's most likely you've accumulated all your assets and debts during the partnership. If you married later in life, assets or debts you previously owned are not subject to the division.

Generally, the only time assets or debts are not split down the middle is when there's a prenuptial agreement. This legal document spells out how assets and debts are divided in the event of a divorce and is usually signed when one person is bringing more assets than the other into the marriage. A prenup might outline who gets the house or cottage after a divorce, how much spousal support should be paid, whether the spouse gets a percentage of the other person's investments, and so on.

Creating the separation agreement

For most marriages and common-law relationships, the *separation agreement* is the most important legal document in a divorce. A separation agreement should include the following:

- **Separation date:** This is the date that the marriage effectively ends. Given that most people don't split up on a particular day—it happens over time — you and your ex-partner will have had to agree on a separation date. Any assets gained by either person after this date are theirs.

- **Children:** A separation agreement should also contemplate the care of any dependent children, including custody arrangements and how long this plan will be in place based on the age of the kids. The agreement must also outline how to split child-related expenses, such as summer camp, tutoring, clothing, and education savings. If one person has the kids more than the other and there's income disparity, child support may need to be paid. Calculating the amount can differ from province to province, so make sure your plan is compliant with any local rules.
- **Spousal support:** Spousal support may also need to be factored into the agreement, especially if one person makes more than the other. The amount is determined by the role each person played in the family —maybe you stayed home while your partner went to work — the length of the marriage, the time a lower-income spouse needs to seek employment, and more.
- **Property division:** The agreement outlines who gets the family home, the car, the cottage, and any other assets.

- **Debts:** The agreement also sorts out the division of debts, including car loans, lines of credit, and credit card debts.
- **Pensions and other savings:** RRSPs and TFSAs need to be tallied up as part of the separation and their assets divided. The value of these savings can be transferred between divorcing spouses without incurring tax penalties. So, for example, you could give your former spouse $200,000 from your RRSP without being subject to withdrawal or income tax.

Contribution room doesn't apply, so even if you've maxed out all your space in your RRSP, you can still take the money you receive in a divorce. By the same token, you don't lose any contribution room by transferring money to your spouse.

Dealing with a pension plan is more complex. First, you have to determine the value of your plan, which may take more work than just looking at a statement. Fortunately, your pension plan's administrator should be able to offer a proper valuation to help with your calculations. If you're dividing the pension, you can have it paid out in a lump sum; converted into a LIRA, or locked-in retirement account (similar to an RRSP, but you can't add funds or withdraw funds until retirement); or transferred to a different pension plan. In many cases, the spouse entitled to these assets can remain in the pension plan until retirement.

Covering legal expenses

Unless you and your partner create the separation agreement and, later, get a divorce on your own, you'll need to hire lawyers. Not every divorce involves teams of legal experts, but even if you use lawyers or a mediator to simply rubber-stamp your agreement, you'll have to pay something. The average uncontested divorce in Canada costs around $1,300, and a contested divorce can cost more $12,000. If the two sides go to court, they could pay a lot more —potentially well over $50,000.

You can pay those fees in a few ways:

- **Line of credit:** A line of credit will give you quick access to cash to pay off your legal costs. A line of credit typically has a lower interest rate than a credit card, and you might be able to negotiate a better rate with your bank. There's no timeframe to pay back a line of credit. As we explore in Chapter 7, the sooner you can pay it off the better.
- **Credit cards:** A lot of law firms accept credit card payments. It's an easy and quick way to pay your fees, but make sure you pay off your plastic as quickly as you can.
- **TFSA:** Since any money saved in a TFSA can be withdrawn without getting taxed, consider liquidating some assets to pay your legal fees. You can recontribute those

funds any time after January 1 in the year after the withdrawal.

- **RRSPs:** You can also use money in an RRSP but should do so only as a last resort. You will have to pay tax on that withdrawal. And if you remove money from an RRSP you will not regain that contribution room.

Adjusting to financial changes

Your bank account and day-to-day financial situation might look quite different after a divorce. For instance, you won't see two paycheques going into an account. But you won't see debit charges from your spouse's lunch purchases coming out of a joint account either. You'll also have more control over your money.

Here are some financial moves that could help you during your transition to singlehood:

- **Adjust your budget.** If you follow a household budget, update it to account for reduced income and expenses. For example, you might need to revise travel, grocery, transportation, and certain housing expenses. (Review budgeting in Chapter 4.)
- **Spend conservatively at first.** In the early months of being single, when your new budget has yet to be tested, be more tight-fisted with your expenses. You

might have extra costs, such as legal fees, a bigger mortgage, or a new car loan. And because your single lifestyle isn't fully formed yet, you won't know how much you'll spend on hobbies and entertainment during an average month.

- **Renegotiate expenses.** Reassess recurring expenses, including your cell phone plan, gym membership, and TV and streaming services. (Do you need five movie services, or was your spouse the movie buff?) Then call your service providers and make sure you're getting the right products and services for your new needs. While you're at it, ensure that you're getting the best rate too!
- **Factor in time.** Now that you run your home on your own, dealing with domestic chores might be more time consuming. To keep your life balanced, you might need to spend more for help with cleaning, lawn care, and meals.
- **Put off big financial decisions**. If you have a big financial decision but don't need to make it right away, consider holding off for a while. Get accustomed to your new single situation before making any big moves.
- **Get advice.** Speak to a financial planner to help you budget and see where you stand financially.

Paying or receiving child support

If you have kids, you and your ex have to make a decision about child support. The federal government has guidance for how to calculate child support, and many provinces have their own rules as well. Some places allow you to pay support through your online bank account, just as you'd pay a bill.

If you receive child support, you don't have to declare it on your income. If you pay child support, you can't deduct the payments from your taxes (as of 1997).

That's not the case with spousal support. The person paying spousal support can deduct this amount from their taxes, and the recipient must declare it as income. If the person paying is also paying child support, those payments must be up to date for the spousal support tax deduction to be allowed.

Carrying On after Losing Your Spouse

Losing a loved one can have significant financial implications. The first challenges you'll likely deal with, though, is finding time — and the emotional bandwidth — to deal with paperwork, such as the will and life insurance and RRSP transfers.

If your spouse died without a will *(intestate)*, you'll have to go through a considerable amount of red tape, time, and money to settle the estate. The person's assets will be divided according to provincial law, which often leaves the entire estate to the surviving spouse but could also divide the estate between the spouse and children. Provinces have rules about how much goes to which family members. Being common-law partners or separated can affect the inheritance, too.

If your spouse had a will, the executor of that person's estate will need to do a few things:

Collect documents. Get a statement of death from the funeral home or a death certificate from your province or territory. If the death happened outside Canada, you'll need a death certificate from that jurisdiction's government.

- **Notify various parties.** Report your spouse's passing to various organizations as soon as you can. If your partner was collecting federal benefits, such as Canada Pension Plan (CPP) or Old Age Security (OAS), notify the government. Also instruct the bank and credit card companies to cancel your spouse's cards.
- **Ensure there's an executor.** An executor, estate representative, or estate trustee should have been named in the will. If not, you may need to ask a trusted friend or family member to become executor. That person will deal with many of the administrative and legal issues

related to the estate and be responsible for distributing assets. (Find out more in Chapter 8.)

* **Go through probate.** *Probate* is the legal approval process that confirms the appointment of the executor of the estate and validates the will.

One of your most important tasks is to claim your spouse's life insurance policy, assuming they had one and you're the beneficiary. (A *beneficiary* is the person entitled to your assets when you pass away.) To file a claim, you verify your identity and submit to the insurance company a policy number and proof of death. You can get a payout by cheque or direct deposit as a lump sum or in installments or perhaps in an annuity that gives you a guaranteed amount until you die. The Canada Revenue Agency categorizes a life insurance payout as a gift, so it isn't taxable.

Protecting Your Assets If You Find a Partner

Love — and marriage — might find you again. This time around, though, you'll have a better idea of the effect that coupledom can have on your money. You'll know not only that it can be easier financially to have a new partner with whom you can share expenses and possibly income but also that second-act relationships can end in divorce or death. That's why it's important to protect yourself and your children.

The following can help you keep control over your assets:

- **Prenuptial agreement:** You may be bringing assets into this new relationship that you won't want to split if the relationship ends, such as a pension, RRSP or TFSA savings, a business, a home, or a vacation property. A prenup can stipulate how these assets get divided, if at all, as well as how assets accumulated during a marriage are split. You can draft your own prenup, but you might want to ask for a lawyer's assistance to be sure it contains all the right details.

  Many people don't realize that a prenup can include what happens to assets upon a spouse's death and can require one spouse to leave certain assets to the other partner in their will.

- **Cohabitation agreement:** If you and your new partner decide to move in together rather than get married, you could be considered common-law spouses. As to when common-law kicks in, each province has its own timeframe, from a few months to a few years. You should draft a cohabitation agreement detailing how to divide your assets if you break up or one spouse dies. Again, you can write this agreement on your own, but you might be more successful creating a valid agreement if you work with a lawyer.

- **Wills:** If you remarry, be sure to adjust your will accordingly. This task is especially important if you have children and want to leave them an inheritance. If you don't have a will and pass away before your spouse, your assets could be left to your partner, who may or may not decide to give them their share of your assets. Make sure you and your new spouse update your wills so both estates are organized in case something happens.
- **Beneficiaries:** Typically, the beneficiary is a spouse, but it could be kids, cousins, or friends. When you're remarrying, make sure to update the beneficiaries on your RRSP, TFSA, and insurance policies. You may want to make your new spouse a beneficiary to all or some assets (you can designate a percentage to different people), or you can designate your children as beneficiaries. We dive into estate planning in Chapter 8.

7

Digging Your Way Out of Debt

We've all had that moment of shock when looking at a credit card statement or line-of-credit balance — the one where we wonder how the heck the number at the bottom got so big. It's normal to spend more money some months and less during others, but if what you owe keeps growing with each passing month, it's time to do something about it.

Of course, debt isn't a single person's problem — almost everyone goes through a period of indebtedness at some point in their lives, often around a major life event that requires a significant outlay of cash, such as the birth of a child, moving, or taking a big trip. Divorce and death, two of the biggest life changes, can precipitate an increasing debt load, too.

Debt can creep up for any number of reasons, and although tackling it on your own can be challenging, it's absolutely achievable. But first, let's understand how debt can pile up in the first place.

Getting Out of a Debt Spiral

Given debt's emotional and financial toll — many studies have found a correlation between debt and depression — you'd think the financial industry would try and limit the amount of money people can borrow. If only. When it comes to how financial institutions view debt, the saying "the more, the merrier" comes to mind. Think about the number of stores that offer a 10 percent discount on your purchase if you apply for their credit card. It's also easy to get a line of credit, tap into your home equity, or take out reverse mortgage.

Financial companies are big on debt because of the interest they collect on your loans. It's essentially free money for them. For instance, if you don't pay off everything you owe every month on your credit card — and the credit card companies are betting you won't — you'll get hit with a hefty interest charge. Most rewards credit cards come with a 20 percent annual interest rate, which means you'll get hit with a $400 payment if you carry a $2,000 balance for the year. The more credit they give you, the more you could potentially borrow and the more interest you might pay.

Understanding how debt piles up

It's easy to find yourself in a debt spiral. Issues can start innocuously enough. Perhaps you put a new flatscreen TV on your credit card, with the thought that you'd pay it off by the end of the month, but then your furnace broke down and you had to put that repair on your credit card too. Now you have a big balance that's hard to pay off in full. So you start making smaller payments, but because you haven't paid the entire balance, interest starts accumulating, which means your bill starts getting a bit bigger. Meanwhile, you're putting new day-to-day purchases on the card, as well as one-time items like the last-minute trip you decided to take with friends. Before you know it, you're deep in debt.

You can see from this scenario how easy it is for debt to accumulate. A car breakdown here, a roof repair there, plus a few too many nights out can suddenly make a credit card or line-of-credit balance balloon. Ultimately, indebtedness happens because of one main issue: You're borrowing more money than you have at your disposal. If you had enough cash to cover all your expenses, you wouldn't need to borrow money.

As discussed in the next section, debt isn't always a bad thing. But if you don't have the cash flow to pay for your purchases, your debt load will increase. And depending on the size of the gap between your expenses and your income, that debt can rise quickly.

Divorced and bereaved individuals are also more prone to racking up debt, at least initially. Separation and death are so difficult emotionally that many people take a leave of absence from work, which then hampers their ability to stay in the black. Getting spousal support or a life insurance payment takes time, and if you're weren't working, you may not have income to pay for your expenses. Other expenses, such as lawyers' fees and moving costs, can add up too.

Ultimately, debt isn't just a matter of overspending. You also need to get your household balance sheet in order and ensure that that you have enough cash coming in to cover what's going out.

Knowing what to pay off first

As mentioned, not all debt is evil. Without debt, most people couldn't own a home, buy a car, go to university, or start a business. As long as you're aware of what you owe and have a plan to pay it off, debt can help you accomplish many of your biggest dreams.

Debt is generally categorized into two buckets: good debt and bad debt. *Good debt* is tied to an appreciating asset or an investment, anything that will eventually make you more money in the future. Debt that supports your ability to earn more money, such as education, also tends to fall in the good debt category.

Here's a list of what's considered good debt:

- **The mortgage on your primary residence:** In theory, there's no better debt than your mortgage. Given that housing prices appreciate over the long term (and often the short term), whatever you eventually sell the house for will net you a nice lump sum. And the price appreciation should cover all the interest payments you made over the years.

  For instance, an $800,000 mortgage on a $1 million home paid off over 25 years at an average 2.5 percent interest rate will generate $275,118 in total interest. That's a lot of interest! But consider this: The average price for a home in Canada has climbed 453 percent over the last 25 years. If your $1 million house climbed by that much over the next 25 years, your abode would be worth $5.53 million, and you'd bank far more than what you paid in interest. If the price of your home rises by a more modest 100 percent to $2 million, you'd still have recouped your interest payments and then some. (Gains made from a home are not subject to tax, which means you keep everything you earn from a sale.)

  Of course, there's no guarantee that prices will continue rising, and increasing interest rates will result in higher interest payments, which could then reduce your total return, but you get the picture. Mortgage debt not only allows you to buy a more expensive home, which could then net a bigger return, but also gives you shelter, which you need to live.

- **Mortgage debt on a secondary residence:** Mortgage debt on another residence can be another good use of debt, assuming real estate continues to rise in value. If you earn rental income on a second property, you not only have price appreciation but also earn a monthly income, which can go towards paying off the mortgage more quickly. In addition, and this is significant, interest paid on the mortgage of a second property, as long as it's used to earn rental or business income, is eligible for a tax deduction. However, you'll get taxed on the eventual sale of a second property — currently half the gain is subject to tax — which will lower your return. Still, you could earn more than the tax and interest combined if housing prices continue to climb.
- **Education:** A lot of people take out student loans to pay for their education. As frustrating as those payments may be, borrowing for school is considered good debt because it allows you to earn more money in the future. In theory, those loans should let you to make a lot more money over your lifetime — more than the cost of school and any interest payments. Now, this isn't as cut and dry as real estate. An MBA, for instance, can cost upwards of $120,000, and there's no guarantee that

your salary will increase enough to earn a return on that investment. And not every profession comes with a six-figure salary, which means it could take a lot longer for you to pay off your student loan than your hotshot lawyer friend. Still, most people need some sort of post-secondary schooling to earn anything, and university is still cheaper in Canada than it is in the U.S.

- **Borrowing to invest in a RRSP:** A lot of people borrow money to top up their RRSP. It's a smart idea for two reasons. First, your assets will earn more money than what you'll spend servicing your debt (at least at the time of writing, with interest rates at low levels). Second, you'll lower your tax rate by a larger amount than you would have if you didn't maximize your RRSP payments, which could result in a larger tax refund.

  Warning: Don't do this if you don't have the money to pay the loan back. If you don't return what you borrowed within a year, the interest payments will start eating into your returns, which then makes the exercise pointless. As well, interest is not tax-deducible on loans used for RRSP or TFSA investing.

- **Borrowing to invest in a non-registered account:** Some people borrow to buy securities for their non-registered account. Again, do this only if you can pay back the loan and you think the return you'll make will be greater than the interest you'll pay. Interest on these loans is tax deductible, which will help you reduce your overall taxable income.

- **Car loan:** We put a car loan in both the good debt and bad categories. For now, it fits in the former because not having a car could affect your ability to earn an income.

Now let's talk about bad debts, which are loans that typically carry high interest rates or are used on depreciating assets. The following is considered bad debt:

- **Credit card debt:** Mortgage debt is the best kind of good debt, and credit card debt is the worst kind of bad debt. Yes, you might need to go into credit card debt at some point in your life, but the interest rates on plastic are usually so high — much higher than the rate you get on good debt — that it doesn't take long for that $10,000 trip to cost another $2,000. Let these debts accumulate and you could end up owing much more than what you paid for the item you put on your credit card. Credit card interest rates typically range from 10 to 25 percent. While credit cards let us buy things without having to carry a wad of cash, they work only if you can pay off the balance in the same month you made the purchases.

- **Line-of-credit (LoC) debt:** Although a line of credit usually has a lower rate than a credit card, an LoC is still typically used to buy things that aren't appreciating in value. Many people use LoCs to fill cash flow gaps or to cover a large purchase. This approach is okay for a month or two, but if your LoC is climbing, you're likely spending more than you're making.
- **Car loan:** A car loan is considered not only a good debt but also a bad debt because a vehicle is a depreciating asset. If you sell your car, you'll get less back than you paid for it. Do you need that $80,000 Tesla to get to work, or will a $20,000 Hyundai do? At a certain price point, the bad debt outweighs the good.

Knowing which debts are good and which are bad is important when figuring out which loans to pay off first. Without question, get rid of your credit balance as soon as you can because those high rates could put you in a debt spiral. In fact, pay down that debt before you save or invest, too. You'll earn more by paying off your 20 percent debt than you will by making 5 percent in the market.

After you've paid off your credit card and line-of-credit debt in full, you'll want to pay off your car loan, your education, and finally your mortgage. Plan to pay off all major debts by the time you retire; after you stop earning a regular income, it can become a lot harder to cover your loans.

TIP One of the most common personal finance questions is whether to use excess cash to pay down a mortgage or invest in the market. (You pay your mortgage every month — we're talking about whether to pay it down faster.) The answer depends on returns and interest rates. If your mortgage rate is 2 percent but you can earn 5 percent in the market, put your money in your RRSP or TFSA. If your mortgage rate is 5 percent but your investment return is lower, you'll make more by paying down your mortgage.

Use this concept with other debt, too. If you'll end up paying more in interest than the return your portfolio can generate, reduce your debt before investing.

Another factor to consider when deciding whether to invest or pay down good debt: How comfortable are you with debt? Some people enjoy the routine of paying a steady amount on their mortgage and seeing their balance decrease, while others prefer seeing their investment portfolio grow. If holding a large debt makes you uncomfortable, pay that down first.

Paying off debt as a single person

Just as all the money a single person makes is their own, all the debt they accumulate is their own, too. If you find yourself drowning in debt, you can bring your head above water in several ways:

- **Create a budget.** As we said, credit card debt piles up when you're spending more than you earn. So the best way to fix this issue is to match your income with your expenses. Do that by budgeting, which we detail in Chapter 4. Track exactly how much money comes and goes out each month and in what spending categories, and then adjust your budget for each one. Also make sure to have a budget line for debt repayment. Look at how much you owe and how quickly you can reasonably pay back your credit card loans without having to cut back on key expenses (such as groceries and shelter), and then make sure you're putting money toward reducing those card payments every month.
- **Consolidate your debts.** A lot of people carry debt from different financial institutions and with varying interest rates. This situation can make it difficult to keep track of what you owe, but it also might make you wonder why you can't just pay the same interest rate on all your loans. Well, perhaps you can. A lot of people with sizable debts from multiple companies take out a consolidation loan.

With a *consolidation loan*, the institution automatically pays off your credit card and line-of-credit debts. (Cut these cards afterwards or you may be tempted to start using them again, especially if they now have a zero balance.) They then charge you one monthly payment, usually at a lower interest rate than what you were paying before (often between 5 and 10 percent). Most require you to pay off the loan over a certain amount of time, such as five years. If you don't, the rate on that debt could rise or the company could go after you for payment. Typically, only people with good credit scores can access this kind of loan.

- **Pay off higher-rate debt with lower-rate ones.** This strategy is a bit like do-it-yourself consolidating. If your credit card rate is 20 percent and your line-of-credit rate is 4 percent, pay off your credit card with your line of credit. You'll still need to pay off the LoC, but at least your interest payments won't be as exorbitant and more of each payment can go towards reducing your principle.
- **Add extra payments.** Try to find ways to redirect more money toward paying down your debts. Perhaps you can temporarily switch your $200-a-month gym membership to a $15-a-month workout app and use that $185 to pay your loans. You'll not only beat your

own repayment schedule but also pay less in interest overall.

Turning to a professional

Sometimes, you simply have more debt than you can deal with on your own. That's okay! It's hard to manage money, and one rough patch can derail even the best laid financial plans.

To help you sort out what to do, consider talking to a debt counsellor or licensed insolvency trustee. These people are trained to help individuals in circumstances just like yours. Let's look at the difference between the two:

- **Accredited not-for-profit credit counsellors.** You can find numerous credit counselling agencies, but those with charitable status aren't looking to profit from your financial troubles. These counsellors will speak with you one-on-one and recommend the best course of action for your situation, whether that's a debt management plan or moving to a licensed insolvency trustee. They may also offer classes on various financial topics.
- **Licensed insolvency trustees.** If your debt is simply too high to repay, it might be time to consider filing for bankruptcy. An insolvency trustee is government regulated and works with you to determine whether you should file a consumer proposal or file for bankruptcy.

They act as a go-between for you and all your creditors and, should you go with a consumer proposal, will act as guarantor for your payments.

Plenty of online resources can help you find a qualified credit counsellor:

- Credit Counselling Canada: `https://creditcounsellingcanada.ca`
- Canadian Association of Credit Counselling Services: `https://financialfitness.ca`
- Canadian Association of Independent Credit Counselling Agencies: `https://caicca.org/`

Because licensed insolvency trustees are federally regulated, the best place to find one in your area is on the government of Canada's website at `www.ic.gc.ca/app/osb/tds/search`.

Submitting a consumer proposal versus filing for bankruptcy

At some point, your debt burden may become so great that you need to either submit a consumer proposal or file for bankruptcy. Both options can be filed only by a licensed insolvency trustee. We can't tell you which one is better, but your trustee will help you decide. Here's a quick comparison.

When filing a consumer proposal:

- Your debt must not exceed $250,000.
- You and your trustee figure out a percentage of your total debt that you're able to repay, and the trustee negotiates this repayment with your creditors.
- You have up to five years to pay the agreed-upon amount.
- Your credit score is negatively affected by the proposal for three years after you've finished all your payments.
- You can keep your assets.

When filing for bankruptcy:

- You must be unable to repay *any* of what you owe.
- Some of your assets may be seized and used toward your debts.
- Your credit score is negatively affected for seven years after filing.
- Your wages will be garnished for up to 21 months if you earn over a predetermined amount.

While the insolvency remains on your credit report (three years after you've completed payments for a consumer proposal, and seven years after filing for bankruptcy), you can take steps to reestablish your credit and begin to improve your credit score.

Increasing Your Credit Score

Several factors affect your credit score. A low rating could be the result of a specific event, such as a bankruptcy, or consistently late or missed payments. Although credit bureaus and financial institutions have their own formulas when assigning scores, the following list can give you a general sense of the importance of each factor in your credit score. Understanding which factors have the biggest effect can help you determine what to focus on when you're rehabilitating your credit score:

- **35 percent for your payment history:** Of course, if you've been consistently late paying any of your bills or missing payments altogether, your credit will drop.
- **30 percent for the total amount you owe:** Your total debt across all accounts plays a significant role, as well as how much credit you're using versus how much is available to you.
- **15 percent for the length of your credit history:** A person who's had one credit card for six months has a lower score in this section than someone who's had a number of cards over 20 years. The former has less of a repayment history for lenders to consider.

- **10 percent for new credit applications:** Applying for too many loans (credit cards, lines of credit, or auto loans) within a year can raise red flags because it looks like you can't properly manage your finances.
- **10 percent for the different types of credit you're using:** As mentioned, not all debt is equal. While this category is the least important facet of your credit score, it's still worth noting that having a bunch of credit card loans does not have the same positive effect as having a mortgage.

Rebuilding your credit is often a slow process. You need to show lenders that you can handle your money, whether you're paying bills or paying off loans. Here are some ways to rebuild your score:

- Set up automatic withdrawals for recurring bill payments so you don't have to worry about remembering to pay bills on time.
- Prioritize your debt. Pay off the bad loans first and increase the repayment amount every month to get rid of your debt as quickly as possible.
- Try to pay off your credit card balances in full each month.
- Keep your credit utilization below 35 percent. In other words, try not to use more than that percentage of your total available credit.

- If you have older credit cards that you're not currently using, keep your accounts open. It may sound counterintuitive, but the unused credit can help lower your debt-to-credit ratio. (Cut up old cards if you're tempted to use them, or close the account if you really can't hold back from putting more debt on your plastic.)

Rebuilding credit takes effort, but slow and steady wins the race. Soon, you'll be back to a high credit rating.

Dealing with Debt after a Loved One Passes Away

It's not uncommon for a spouse to find out after their partner passes away that their loved one was deep in debt. If you weren't the one looking after the family finances, you may not have any idea how much credit card debt has been accumulating. Or you could be well aware of the debt your family is carrying, but are now worried about how you're going to pay it off on a single income.

If you're concerned about the debt your spouse has left behind, here's some good news: You're not responsible for paying it off. That doesn't mean the debts get wiped out, though. Rather, the estate has to settle those payments before any assets go to you or other beneficiaries. (This doesn't include life insurance, which bypasses the estate with a named beneficiary — more on this topic in Chapter 8.) If the credit card debt is greater than the value of the estate's assets, that debt disappears. The one exception is if the credit card was opened in two people's names — so you would have been a co-signer on the card (this is different than having a second credit card with your name on it). In this case, you would be liable to pay off any outstanding amounts.

If your spouse has passed away and you're still paying off the mortgage, you'll have to continue paying back that loan. The house is now probably in your name — it was either given to you in your partner's will or in both of your names to start with — so it's now your sole responsibility.

Curbing the Urge to Overspend after a Divorce

We cover the nitty-gritty on divorce finances in Chapter 6 — remember that debts usually get split down the middle, just like assets. But on the other side of your divorce papers lies a new temptation: spending beyond your means. No one doubts that you deserve a trip to a tropical island to celebrate being newly single; just make sure to save for it first.

Retail therapy is not an uncommon behaviour after a divorce. After all, you're probably dealing with many emotions, and a few indulgences can make you feel better, albeit temporarily. But as mentioned, if you find yourself overspending for more than a month or two, it could be the start of your very own debt spiral.

A few other factors can lead to overspending, post-divorce:

- **Lifestyle expectations:** You may have lived the high life as a married couple because your spouse made a lot of money and freely spent the cash. Now that you're living on one income, you might have to slow down the spending. This process can be difficult — spending money is easy — so stick to your budget as much as you can.
- **Living expenses:** As mentioned in Chapter 4, many living expenses are easier to manage on two incomes. For instance, you'll likely have the same heating bills and property taxes even if one person has moved out. If those expenses get too hard to manage, you might need to downsize your living space and, as a result, your bills.

Whatever your single situation may be, the best thing you can do to avoid falling into a debt spiral is to create a budget that you can stick to and pay down any existing debts as quickly as possible.

8

Leaving a Legacy

No one likes to think about their own mortality, but if you want to make sure your assets are left to your loved ones or perhaps to your favourite charity, you need think about how you wish to divide your assets and possessions after you pass away. This kind of planning is called legacy planning because it's your last chance to leave your mark on the world.

Legacy planning requires you to ask yourself some weighty questions: What kind of lasting impression do you want to leave on people? How do you want to be remembered? What kind of change can you make before you go? In this chapter, we look at what's involved with leaving a legacy.

Taking Care of Your Money When You No Longer Need It

It's not easy to think about what should happen with your money after you pass away, but it's important that you do so. Otherwise, your provincial court will determine it for you. The last thing you want is for family members to fight over your assets or for the court to do something against your wishes. Ensuring that your money is disbursed the way you want involves a few tasks, such as creating a will, developing an estate plan, and naming beneficiaries on your investment accounts.

The process is best done with a financial advisor or planner. But before you begin that process, reflect on the legacy you want to leave behind:

- **Think about your desires.** You could simply leave your assets to your children, which might help them save for their future or pay off their mortgage. If you don't have kids, you might have close family members or friends you'd like to help. You might also want to leave a chunk of change to favourite charities. Think about your final wishes and how you want your money to get distributed and spent after you pass away. After you make those decisions, put your desires in your will.

- **Gather your documents**. Put your various financial documents in one place so that your executor has easy access to everything needed to administer your estate. These documents include your will, life insurance policies, and RRSP and TFSA statements, the name of your financial advisor, and pension plan information.
- **Talk to the experts.** If you have a more complicated estate — maybe you're leaving behind a thriving business or you have assets outside Canada — talk to a financial advisor and perhaps other experts, such as a lawyer and an accountant, to ensure that those assets can be transferred or liquidated without any issues.

After you know what you want to do with your money and have gathered all your documents, consider telling the recipients what you're bequeathing so there's no confusion or fighting after you've passed away. Here's what to do as part of that discussion:

- **Discuss the necessary documents.** Now that you have your documents organized, make sure everyone has access to a copy. Walk through the details of your plans so your family knows what tasks must be completed after you pass away, such as claiming life insurance.
- **Gather everyone and share your wishes.** Telling people what they're getting before they find out in your will is a good way to stave off potential problems, especially

when your children are involved. Have this discussion as early as you can, not later when you might be sick. Maybe the older child loves the cottage more than the younger ones — tell everyone that the eldest gets the second home but has to pay the siblings their share of the abode.

- **Sort out any issues.** If there's a disagreement as to how assets should be divided, work it out with all involved. This task is easier said than done, especially with something as emotional as death. If you expect a fraught conversation, hire a financial advisor who can bring a fresh and objective perspective to the discussion.

Get your plans communicated and settled in advance. You don't want to worry about family fighting while you're trying to make the most of your final days.

Deciding Who Gets What with a Will

According to Legalwills.ca, only about 40 percent of Canadians have a will, which is a low number given that this is one of the most important legal documents you can create in your lifetime. Creating a will doesn't have to take weeks; you can do so in a few days or even a few hours, depending on the complexity of your estate.

Most people can hire a lawyer to write a will for less than $1,000. And online sites, such as `www.willful.com`, can help you create a legally binding document for as little as $99. Consider a lawyer if you want to create a will with more nuance and detail; online sites work best for those with more straightforward wishes.

The first step to creating a will is to think about who should get your assets and belongings. Here are the most common beneficiaries:

- **Children:** If you have children, you'll most likely leave most of your estate to them. The easiest way to do this is to divide your assets evenly between all your kids. But this approach won't work for all families. What if one child is better off than another? Do you give the child who needs more money a larger share of the estate? How will that make the other children feel? What if one child isn't as financially responsible as the others? In that case, you might set up a trust that dictates how an inheritance can be used. If you have a large estate, you might be wary of giving your kids everything and risk having them use your funds to get through life rather than relying on their own hard work. To broach these topics with your kids, you might want to bring in an advisor or even a therapist.
- **Charity:** An increasing number of people are leaving large sums to charity, such as a hospital, alma matter,

religious centre, and other organizations that have touched their lives. This option is great for a few reasons. Your wealth can help people for years to come as well as reduce the tax on your estate. If you donate money after your death, your estate will receive a tax receipt — just like you do now when you donate — which can reduce the amount of income tax your estate must pay.

- **Friends and other family:** If you don't have children, consider leaving your assets to other loved ones. You might help fund a young relative's university education — say in your will that you want a certain dollar amount to go into the person's RESP (registered education savings plan) — or first home. You could do the same with the children of a close friend or confidant.

The next step is to think about what you want to leave behind. Here are some of the assets typically accounted for in a will.

- **Money:** Cash and investments top the list of assets that are passed down, including money in an RRSP or a TFSA and remaining pension dollars and funds in bank accounts. Investments are usually sold after the owner passes away and then transferred as cash.

- **Possessions with sentimental value:** Specify who gets your prized possessions, such as a grandmother's wedding ring or your signed Guy Lafleur hockey card. These decisions are more complicated than splitting money equally and can lead to hurt feelings. What if two kids treasure the wedding ring or hockey card? Again, talk openly about which assets family members and friends want or will receive.
- **Real estate and other tangible assets:** If you own a home when you pass away, your estate will probably end up selling the house and distributing the proceeds to your beneficiaries. But what if one of your children wants to live in the home? And who gets the cottage by the lake or the condo in Florida? Ensuring that these assets and others are distributed in accordance with your wishes is an essential part of legacy planning.

It's important to understand how assets can be owned so that you leave them to the right person. There are two ways that ownership can be structured:

- **Joint with right of survivorship:** This structure covers assets jointly owned by you and another person. If you pass away before the co-owner of the asset, your share passes to that person, who becomes the sole owner of the asset.

- **Tenants-in-common:** In this case, you still own the asset with another person, but you can choose to leave your share to someone else after you pass away.

The best will is one in which your wishes are communicated clearly. Don't leave room for interpretation — you'll open up your estate to fighting and legal challenges.

Bequeathing Life Insurance

We've talked about life insurance throughout the book in the context of a spouse claiming a life insurance policy after their significant other passes away. Generally, people take out a life insurance policy to replace the income that can no longer be earned when someone passes away. A spouse earning $200,000 a year might take out a $2 million life insurance policy to ensure that their surviving partner has a decade's worth of dollars to live on. Some people take out enough to pay off their mortgage so that their spouse doesn't have to worry about paying off the family's biggest expense. Single people with young children might leave the policy to the person who will be looking after their children (if the other parent is not in the picture).

If you don't need insurance to replace your income — perhaps you don't have children or they're older and making their own living — you don't need life insurance. However, single people might still want to take out a policy to do the following:

- **Pay estate taxes:** If you have investments in an RRSP or RRIF or a second property that must be sold, your estate must pay taxes on the sale. Depending on the value of your assets, the bill could be hefty. You could pay the bill with the proceeds from selling your assets, but you might use up most of the money. Instead, pay the bill by using life insurance, which isn't taxable, and then pass down the remaining funds to your beneficiaries.
- **Give to charities:** Many big donations to schools, churches, or foundations are made not with cash from a bank account but with a life insurance policy. If you want to support an organization, take out a life insurance policy and make the organization the beneficiary. When you pass away, your estate will receive a tax receipt for the amount of the policy, which can then be used to reduce your estate's tax bill.
- **Leave money to loved ones:** A life insurance policy is also a great way ensure that the people you care about get something after you pass away. Just hoping you'll have money to leave to someone doesn't always work, and a large portion might end up going to tax. With life insurance, as long as you pay the monthly or annual premium (which can get

expensive as you get older), your loved ones will get a lump sum payout.

TIP

Taking out life insurance is a savvy financial move because you generally pay a lot less per month over the lifetime of the policy than what will be paid out. For instance, say tax on the estate is $1 million. Your policy for that same amount costs $300 a month. Pay that over 30 years and you've spent $108,000 for a $1 million payment. If you didn't have an insurance policy, you would have to pay the $1 million tax bill out of the estate.

Estate Planning for Singles

Although everyone should take estate planning seriously, if a couple doesn't have a plan, in most cases the assets are simply transferred to the surviving spouse. When you're single, estate planning is even more important. Remember, if you don't convey your intentions, the courts will likely decide for you.

Estate planning shouldn't be a one-and-done activity. Revisit your will and other estate documents annually, especially after a life change such as separation, divorce, death, or remarriage. Too many estates have gone sideways because of incomplete, old, or missing information. For example, if you don't update your will after a divorce, your ex-spouse could be legally entitled to your assets, even if you've been apart for decades.

Too many estates end up in court, and disputes between beneficiaries and family are one of the primary reasons why estates often take a long time to settle. Contesting a will should be done only after seeking legal advice. According to LegalWills.ca (`www.legalwills.ca`), about 74 percent of contested wills are settled in favour of the family. (The rest are settled in favour of a public trustee or executor or other third-party.) Being clear about your intentions is the primary way of avoiding a court battle, but you should also appoint an executor who can make sure your assets are properly distributed.

Appointing an executor

An *executor* is the person responsible for managing your estate. The executor's role is to ensure that each person gets what they're entitled to and your debts are paid. When choosing an executor, pick someone who is trustworthy — you want them to follow your instructions to the letter — is likely to outlive you, and lives nearby to resolve issues that may arise. Executors are paid about 5 percent of the value of the estate, though they could choose to forgo that payment.

Parents often choose one of their kids to be executor. That's all well and good if you have only one child or your kids get along. But this approach might cause problems if your children don't like each other, your child doesn't want the responsibility, especially when they're grieving, or your child lives far away. Other options for executor include a trusted friend, another family member, or a professional employed by a trust company or financial firm.

Regardless of the person you choose, the executor must have the right capabilities. After all, you're giving that person the power to act on your behalf. In addition, remember that settling an estate might require weeks or months of work.

Choosing a power of attorney

As you've created a will and pondered who might be your executor, think about naming a power of attorney for health and another for financial issues, though they could be the same person. These people will make financial and health decisions for you if you can't make them for yourself. If you're incapacitated, for instance, you'll need someone who can communicate with your doctors on your behalf. You'll also need a person to make financial decisions for you, which could include continuing to pay your bills or spending money on additional healthcare needs. As with an executor, make sure you choose someone you trust — if you can't communicate, you won't have a say in what happens next. A power of attorney is often a family member but can be a friend or another trusted person in your circle.

About the Authors

Julie Shipley-Strickland is a certified financial planner with nearly 15 years of industry experience, currently serving as a senior wealth advisor with Wellington-Altus Private Wealth in Alberta, Canada. Often described as passionate, forthright, and dynamic, Julie builds strong relationships with her valued clients by understanding their goals, supporting their concerns, and producing thoughtful and strategic solutions. Julie has been frequently interviewed and quoted in publications such as the *Globe and Mail* and *Maclean's* magazine. She also regularly interviews for several Canadian-based lifestyle podcasts, where she customarily shares the story of her entrepreneurial journey and provides timely financial insights to fellow business owners and professional executives.

As a successful investment and insurance advisor, Julie paves the way for future females in finance with her dedication to supporting female entrepreneurs and business owners, serving as an advisor on the Women of Wellington Advisory council, and launching her self-created video-led financial literacy e-course entitled the Wealth with Julie Prosperity Playbook, which is designed to support this community further and foster the development of wealth-building rituals. In addition, Julie currently serves as treasurer on the board of GROW by EO YYC (formerly EOA) and routinely volunteers her time with Junior Achievement of Southern Alberta. On a daily basis, Julie provides independent investment advice, financial planning, insurance solutions, and clear guidance to entrepreneurs, executives, and their families. A family woman herself, Julie lives in Calgary, Alberta, with her husband, two children, and their dog Bentley.

Bryan Borzykowski is an award-winning business journalist who has been writing about investing and finance for well over a decade. He's written for the *New York Times,* CNBC, BBC Capital, the *Washington Post, Wired,* the *Globe and Mail,* MoneySense, and many others. He is also the founder and editorial director of ALLCAPS Content (`www.allcapscontent.com`), an agency that helps businesses and organizations create editorial-style content, has written several personal finance books, including *ETFs For Canadian For Dummies,* and appears regularly on CTV News Channel and SiriusXM radio. Bryan was the president of the Society for Advancing Business Editing and Writing, an international organization of business journalists, and is the current president of the Canadian Jewish News. Bryan lives in Winnipeg with his wife, three daughters, and two dogs.